THE

# CONCHOLOGIST'S FIRST BOOK:

OR,

## A SYSTEM

OF

## TESTACEOUS MALACOLOGY,

Arranged expressly for the use of Schools,

IN WHICH

THE ANIMALS, ACCORDING TO CUVIER, ARE GIVEN
WITH THE SHELLS,

A GREAT NUMBER OF NEW SPECIES ADDED,

AND THE WHOLE BROUGHT UP, AS ACCURATELY AS POSSIBLE, TO
THE PRESENT CONDITION OF THE SCIENCE.

---

### BY EDGAR A. POE.

---

WITH ILLUSTRATIONS OF TWO HUNDRED AND FIFTEEN SHELLS,
PRESENTING A CORRECT TYPE OF EACH GENUS.

PHILADELPHIA:

PUBLISHED FOR THE AUTHOR, BY

HASWELL, BARRINGTON, AND HASWELL,

AND FOR SALE BY THE PRINCIPAL BOOKSELLERS IN THE
UNITED STATES.

**1129. Poe (Edgar Allan).** The Conchologist's Text-Book, with a glossary of tecn
cal terms. By Capt. Thomas Brown. With 19 plates on steel. 12mo original printe
ards, 180 pp. Glasgow, 1833. Bookplate. **$10.0**
Very scare. The first issue of the book said to have been plagarized by Poe and put
;hed. Phila., 1839. See "International Magazine", Oct. 1850. Binding worn but clea
py inside, edges untrimmed.

# PREFACE.

THE term " *Malacology,*" an abbreviation of " *Mala-
coxoology,*" from the Greek μαλακος, *soft,* ζωον, *an animal,*
and λογος, *a discourse,* was first employed by the French
naturalist De Blainville to designate an important division of Natural History, in which the leading feature of
the animals discussed was the *softness* of the flesh, or,
to speak with greater accuracy, of the general envelop.
This division comprehends not only the *mollusca,*
but also the *testacea* of Aristotle and of Pliny, and, of
course, had reference to molluscous animals in general
—of which the greater portion have shells.

A treatise concerning the shells, exclusively, of this
greater portion, is termed, in accordance with general
usage, a Treatise upon Conchology or Conchyliology ;
although the word is somewhat improperly applied, as
the Greek *conchylion,* from which it is derived, embraces in its signification both the animal and shell.
Ostracology would have been more definite.

The common works upon this subject, however, will
appear to every person of science very essentially
defective, inasmuch as the *relations* of the animal and
shell, with their dependence upon each other, is a
radically important consideration in the examination of
either. Neither, in the attempt to obviate this difficulty,
is a work upon Malacology at large necessarily included.
Shells, it is true, form, and for many obvious reasons,

will continue to form, the subject of chief interest whether with regard to the school or the cabinet. There is no good reason why a book upon *Conchology* (using the common term) may not be malacological as far as it proceeds.

In this view of the subject the present little work is offered to the public. Beyond the ruling feature—that of giving an anatomical account of each animal, together with a description of the shell which it inhabits, the Author has aimed at little more than accuracy and simplicity, as far as the latter quality can be thought consistent with the rigid exactions of science.

No attention has been given to the mere *History* of our subject; it is conceived that any disquisition on this head would more properly appertain to works of ultimate research, than to one whose sole intention is to make the pupil acquainted, in as tangible a form as possible, with *results*. To afford, at a cheap rate, a concise, yet sufficiently comprehensive, and especially a well illustrated school-book, has been the principal design.

In conclusion, the author has only to acknowledge his great indebtedness to the valuable public labors, as well as private assistance of Mr. Isaac Lea, of Philadelphia. To Mr. Thomas Wyatt, and his late excellent *Manual of Conchology*, he is also under many obligations. No better work, perhaps, could be put into the hands of the student as a secondary text-book. Its beautiful and perfectly well-coloured illustrations afford an aid in the collection of a cabinet scarcely to be met with elsewhere.

E. A. P.

# INTRODUCTION.

---

The term " *Conchology*," in its legitimate usage, is applied to that department of Natural History which has reference to animals with testaceous covering or shells. It is not unfrequently compounded with *Crustaceology*, but the distinction is obvious and radical, lying not more in the composition of the animal's habitation than in the organization of the animal itself. This latter, in the *Crustacea*, is of a fibrous nature, and has articulated limbs; the shell, strictly adapted to the members, covers the creature like a coat of mail, is produced at one elaboration, is cast or thrown aside periodically, and, again at one elaboration, renewed; it is moreover composed of the animal matter with phosphate of lime. In the *Testacea*, on the contrary, the inhabitant is of a simple and soft texture, without bones, and is attached to its domicil by a certain adhesive muscular force; this domicil, too, is a permanent one, and is increased, from time to time, by gradual adhesions on the part of the tenant; while the entire shell, which is distributed in layers, or strata, is a combination of carbonate of lime, with a very small portion of gelatinous matter. Such animals, then, with such shells, form, alone, the subject of a proper " Conchology."

Writers have not been wanting to decry this study as frivolous or inessential; not unjustly assailing the science itself on account of the gross abuses which have now and then arisen from its exclusive and extravagant pursuit. They have reasoned much after this fashion :—that Conchology is a folly, because Rumphius was a fool. The *Conus Cedo Nulli* has been sold for three hundred guineas, and the naturalist just mentioned gave a thousand pounds sterling for one of the first discovered specimens of the *Venus Dione* (of Linnæus). But there have been men in all ages who have carried to an absurd, and even pernicious extreme, pursuits the most ennobling and praiseworthy.

To an upright and well regulated mind, there is no portion of the works of the Creator, coming within its cognizance, which will not afford material for attentive and pleasurable investigation ; and, so far from admitting the venerable error even now partially existing to the discredit of Conchology, we should not hesitate to acknowledge, that while few branches of Natural History are of more direct, *very few* are of more adventitious importance.

Testaceous animals form the principal subsistence of an immense number of savage nations, inhabitants of the sea-board. On the coast of Western Africa, of Chili, of New Holland, and in the clustered and populous islands of the Southern seas, how vast an item is the apparently unimportant shell-fish in the wealth and happiness of man ! In more civilized countries it often supplies the table with a delicate luxury. Nor must we forget the services of the pinna with its web, nor of the purpura with its brilliant and once valuable dye, nor omit to speak of the pearl-oyster, with the radiant nacre, and the *gem* which it produces, and the world of industry which it sets in action as minister to the luxury which it stimulates.

Shells, too, being composed of particles already in natural combination, have not within them, like flowers and animals, the seed of dissolution. While the preparation of a specimen for the cabinet is a simple operation, a conchological collection will yet remain perhaps for ages. These important circumstances being duly considered, in connexion with the universally acknowledged beauty and variety, both of form and color, so strikingly observable in shells, it is a matter for neither wonder nor regret that these magnificent *exuviæ*, even regarded merely as such, should have attracted, in a very exclusive degree, the attention and the admiration of the naturalist. The study of Conchology, however, when legitimately directed, and when regarding these *exuviæ* in their natural point of view, as the habitations, wonderfully constructed, of an immensely numerous and vastly important branch of the animal creation, will lead the mind of the investigator through paths hitherto but imperfectly trodden, to many novel contemplations of Almighty Beneficence and Design.

But it is, beyond all doubt, in a geological point of view that Conchology offers the most of interest to the student; and here, by reference to the fair pages of a profound and mighty knowledge, to which it has pointed out the searcher after truth, are triumphantly refuted all charges brought against it of insignificance or frivolity.

" In fine, the relations of the mollusca," says De Blainville, " with the mineral kingdom, and consequently with the mass of the earth which they contribute to form, are not devoid of interest, for without seeking here to resolve the physiological question— whether the conchyliferous mollusca borrow of the inorganic kingdom the calcareous matter which composes their shells, or whether they form it of themselves, it is still certain that they produce, at least, changes upon the surface of the earth by accumulating this material in some places more than in others, and in consequence that they alter the physiognomy of the superficial structure of the globe, the study of which constitutes geognosy."

" By this," says Parkinson, " we are taught that innumerable beings have lived, of which not one of the same kind does any longer exist—that immense beds composed of the spoils of these animals, extending for many miles under ground, are met with in many parts of the globe—that enormous chains of mountains, which seem to load the surface of the earth, are vast monuments, in which these remains of former ages are entombed—that, though lying thus crushed together, in a rude and confused mass, they are hourly suffering these changes, by which, after thousands of years, they become the chief constituent parts of gems, the limestone which forms the humble cottage of the peasant, or the marble which adorns the splendid palace of the prince." Fossil, wood, coral, and shells, are, indeed, as Bergman has very forcibly remarked, the only true remaining " medals of Creation."

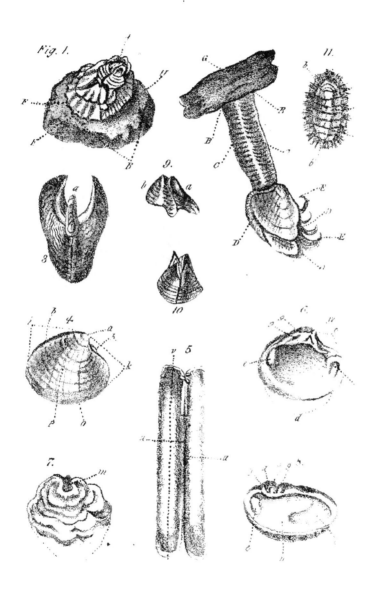

Pl. 2

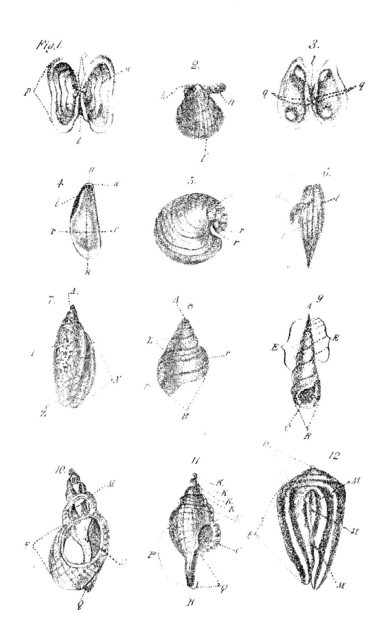

Pl. 3

# Parts of Shells.

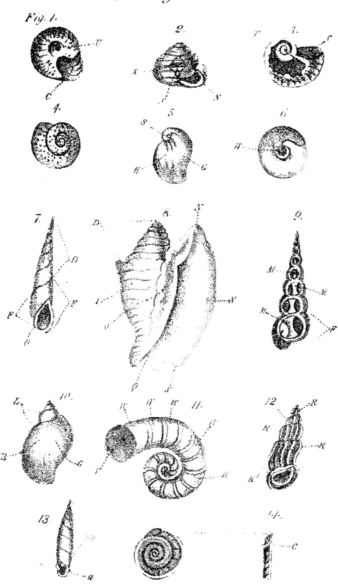

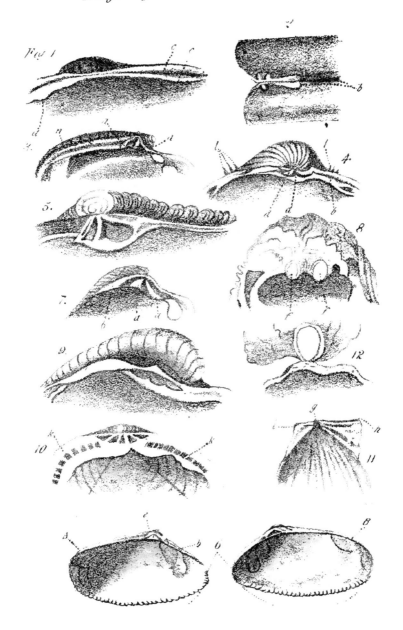

1 Siliquaria. 2 Dentalium. 3 Pectinaria. 4 Sabellaria. 5 Terebella.
6 Amphitrite. 7 Spirorbis. 8 Serpula. 9 Vermilia. 10 Galeolaria.
11 Magilus. 12 Tubicinella. 13 Coronula. 14 Balanus.
15 Acasta. 16 Creusia. 17 Pyrgoma. 18 Anatifera. 19 Pollicipes.
20 Cineras. 21 Otion. 22 Aspergillum.

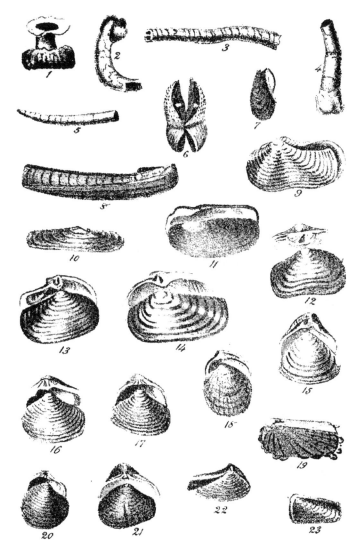

1 Claragella. 2 Fistulana. 3 Septaria. 4 Teredina. 5 Teredo.
6 Pholas. 7 Gastrochaena. 8 Solen. 9 Panopea. 10 Selecur-
tus. 11 Glycimeris. 12 Mya. 13 Anatina. 14 Lutraria.
15 Mactra. 16 Crassatella. 17 Erycina. 18 Ungulina.
19 Solenimya. 20 Amphidesma. 21 Corbula. 22 Pandora.
23 Saxicava.

1 *Petricola*. 2 *Venerirupis*. 3 *Sanguinolaria*. 4 *Psammobia*.
5 *Psammolea*. 6 *Tellina*. 7 *Tellinides*. 8 *Corbis*. 9 *Lucina*.
10 *Donax*. 11 *Capsa*. 12 *Crassina*. 13 *Cyclas*. 14 *Cyrena*.
15 *Galathea*. 16 *Cyprina*. 17 *Cytherea*. 18 *Venus*. 19 *Veneri-
cardia*. 20 *Cardium*. 21 *Cardita*. 22 *Cypricardia*. 23 *Hiatella*.

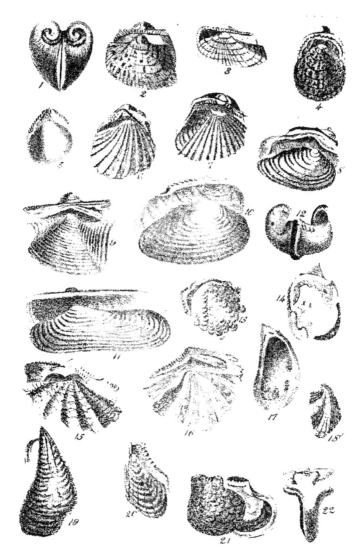

1 Isocardia 2 Cucullea. 3. Arca. 4 Pectunculus. 5. Nucula
6 Trigonia. 7 Castalia. 8 Unio. 9 Myria. 10 Anodonta.
11 Iridina. 12 Diceras. 13 Chama. 14 Etheria. 15 Tridocna
16 Hippopus. 17. Mytilus. 18. Modiola. 19 Pinna.
20 Crenatula. 21 Perna. 22. Matleus.

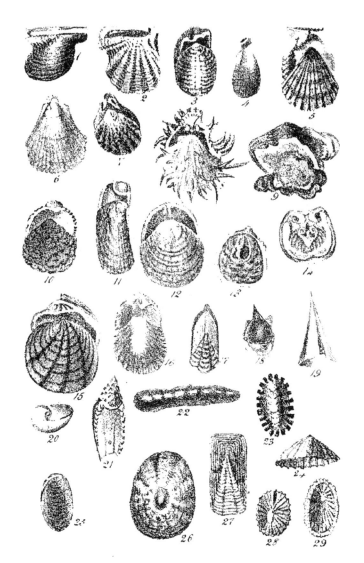

1. *Avicula*. 2 *Meleagrina*. 3 *Pedum*. 4 *Lima*. 5 *Pecten*.
6 *Plagiostoma*. 7 *Plicatula*. 8 *Spondylus*. 9 *Gryphea*.
10 *Ostrea*. 11 *Vulsella*. 12 *Placuna*. 13 *Anomia*. 14 *Crania*.
15 *Orbicula*. 16 *Terebratula*. 17 *Lingula*. 18 *Hyalea*.
19 *Cleodora*. 20 *Limacina*. 21 *Cymbulia*. 22 *Chitonellus*.
23 *Chiton*. 24 *Patella*. 25 *Pleurobranchus*. 26 *Umbrella*.
27 *Parmophorus*. 28 *Emarginula*. 29 *Fissurella*.

P. S. Duval lith.r Phil.a

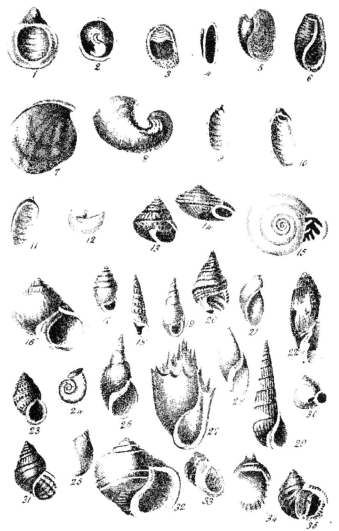

1 *Pileopsis*. 2 *Calyptrea*. 3 *Crepidula*. 4 *Ancylus*. 5 *Bullaea*.
6 *Bulla*. 7 *Aplysia*. 8 *Dolabella*. 9 *Parmacella*. 10 *Limax*.
11 *Testacella*. 12 *Vitrina*. 13 *Helix*. 14 *Carocella*. 15 *Anostoma*.
16 *Helicina*. 17 *Pupa*. 18 *Clausilia* 19 *Bulimus*. 20 *Achatina*.
21 *Succinea*. 22 *Auricula*. 23 *Cyclostoma*. 24 *Planorbis*.
25 *Physa*. 26 *Lymnea*. 27 *Melania* 28 *Melanopsis*.
29 *Pirena*. 30 *Valvata*. 31 *Paludina*. 32 *Ampularia*.
33 *Neritina*. 34 *Navicella*. 35 *Nerita*.

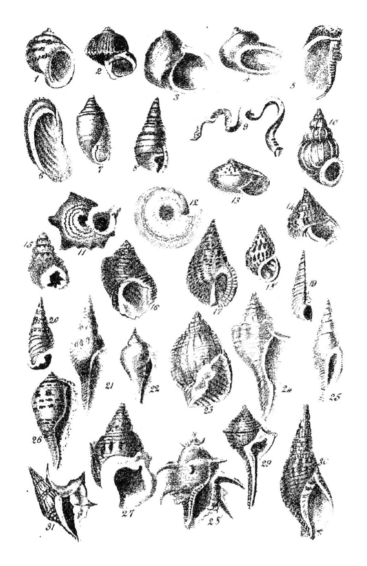

1 Natica. 2 Janthina 3 Sigaretus. 4 Stomatella. 5 Stomatia.
6 Haliotis. 7 Tornatella. 8 Pyramidella. 9 Vermetus. 10 Scalaria.
11 Delphinula. 12 Solarium. 13 Rotella. 14 Trochus. 15 Monodonta.
16 Turbo. 17 Planaxis. 18 Phasianella. 19 Turritella.
20 Cerithium. 21 Pleurotoma. 22 Turbinella. 23 Cancillaria.
24 Fasciolaria. 25 Fusus. 26 Pyrula. 27 Struthiolaria.
28 Ranella. 29 Murex. 30 Triton. 31 Rostellaria.

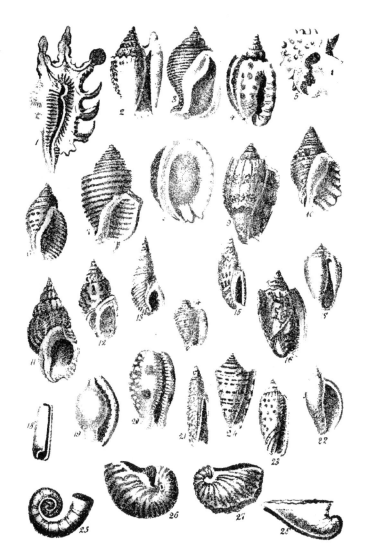

1 Pterocerus. 2 Strombus. 3 Cassidaria. 4 Cassis. 5 Ricinula.
6 Purpura. 7 Monoceros. 8 Concholepas. 9 Harpa. 10 Dolium.
11 Buccinum. 12 Eburna. 13 Terebra. 14 Columbella. 15 Mitra.
16 Voluta 17 Marginella. 18 Volvaria. 19 Ovula. 20 Cyprea.
21 Terebellum. 22 Ancillaria. 23 Oliva. 24 Conus. 25 Spirula.
26 Nautilus. 27 Argonauta. 28 Carinaria.

# EXPLANATION OF THE PARTS OF SHELLS.

## MULTIVALVE.

A MULTIVALVE shell is composed of more parts than two. Every part of a shell which is connected by a cartilage, ligament, hinge, or tooth, is called a valve of such shell; thus the Chitons have eight transverse, broad, but very short valves, placed on the back of the animal, and inserted at their sides into a marginal tough ligament. Plate I. fig. 1. *A A A*.

*Operculum* consists of four small valves on the summit of the lepas, which shut up the superior orifice; it is in a certain degree stationary, and different from the operculum of univalve shells, which will hereafter be described. Plate I. fig. 1. A. Fig. 9. represents a profile view of the operculum removed from its place, *A* the front valves, *B* the back valves. Fig. 10. a front view of the operculum.

*Base*, is that part of the shell by which it is fixed to rocks and other bodies. Plate I. fig. 1. and 2. B B B.—H is a piece of stone to which the base is fixed, and G a piece of wood to which the shells of this section are generally attached.

*Ligament*, is the membranous or tendinous substance by which the valves or parts of the shell are attached. Some multivalve shells are connected by the parts of one valve locking into an other. Plate I. fig. 2. D D D. The ligaments vary considerably in their texture, being scaly, prickly, smooth, or punctated.

*Ridges*, are certain convexities in many of the Lepas tribe, sometimes longitudinal and sometimes transverse. Plate I. fig. 1. F F.

*Peduncle.* A sort of stem by which the shells of the Anatifera are attached to wood, &c. It is a membranaceous substance, similar to a bladder but materially thinner, and filled with a liquid which evidently affords nourishment to the animal. Plate I. fig. 2. c c, the peduncle is usually affixed to a piece of wood as represented at G.

*Feelers*, are those crenated arms, evolved from the side of the Anatifera. While the animal is in the water it continually moves its feelers, evidently for the purpose of entangling minute marine insects, as food. Plate I. fig. 2. E E.

*Accessory Valves*, are small plates which cover the apex at the hinge of the Pholades, or are situated below the hinge. Plate I. fig. 3. *A*.

*Margin.*—A fleshy border in which the valves are attached in the genus Chiton. Plate I. fig. 11. *B B*.

### BIVALVE.

Bivalve shells consist of two parts or valves, connected by a cartilage, and a hinge which is generally composed of teeth; those of the one valve locking into a cavity in the other.

The valves of some bivalve shells are formed exactly alike, and others are very different; the 'one being smooth, the other rugose; one flat and another convex; and often one is shorter than the other.

The shells of the Mya, Solen, Tellina, Venus, and others, have in general both valves alike, while those of the Spondylus, Ostrea, and Anomia, have in general dissimilar valves. The first of these kinds are called equivalve, and the latter inequivalve.

*Equilateral* shells, are those whose sides are alike, as in the shells of the genus Pecten. Plate II. fig. 2. and plate VII. fig. 14. This is also exemplified in the Pectunclus.

*Inequilateral valves*, are shells whose sides are unequal; and of different shapes, as in the Mactra, Donax, &c.

*Summit*, is the most elevated point of that part of the shell in which the hinge is placed. Plate I. fig. 4. and 8. *a a*.

In naming this the summit, we do not follow the axiom of Linnæus, but because we consider it more properly the summit of the shell than the opposite extremity.

*Base*, is the reverse of the above, or that part of the shell immediately opposite the summit. Plate I. fig 6. and 7. *d d*.

*Sides*, the right and left parts of the valves. Plate I. fig. 6. *c*.

*Posterior slope*, is that part of the shell in which the ligament is situated. In viewing the posterior slope in front, the beaks of the shell retire from view. Plate I. fig. 4. *i.*

*Anterior slope,* that part of the shell opposite the posterior slope; in viewing it in front, the beaks point to the observer. Plate I. fig. 4. *k.*

*Disk,* the convex centre of a valve, or most prominent part of the valve, suppose it with its inside lying undermost. Plate I. fig. 4. *o.*

*Inside,* the concave part of a valve. Plate IV. fig. 6. *n.*

*Muscular impression,* is the impression left on the inside of the valves, by the adhering muscles of the animal. It differs in most shells, according to the shape of the animal, as semi-ovate, round, lunate, elongated, &c. As a specific distinction, it is often of great use; being, with a very few exceptions, alike in shells of the same species. Some shells have only one cicatrix, as the Edible Oyster, and Mytilus; others have two, and some few more; the Tellina for example. Plate I. fig. 6. and 8. *e e e e.*

*Lunule.* The lunated depressions, situated in the anterior and posterior slopes. In different species of Venus they are prominent, characteristic marks, often of much service in ascertaining a species. Plate I. fig. 4. *b b.*

*Ligament perforation.* The circular aperture, or perforation through which the ligament passes; by which the animal of the Anomia attaches itself to stones, and other marine extraneous bodies; it is in general situated in the flat valve, though there are a few exceptions to the contrary. Plate I. fig. 7. *m.*

*Hinge,* is the point at which bivalve shells are united, it is formed by the teeth of one valve inserting themselves between those of the other, or by the teeth of one valve fitting into the cavities or sockets of the opposite one.

It is on the peculiar construction of the *hinge* that the generic character of bivalve shells is principally founded, together with the general contour of the shell. Plate II. fig. 1. and 3. *q q q.*

*Teeth of the Hinge.* Upon the number and relative situation of the teeth, principally depend the specific distinctions; they are of various forms, and very differently placed; some are single and large, others numerous and small, orbicular, spatuliform, laminated, &c.  Some hinges have no visible teeth, and are termed *inarticulate.*—When a primary tooth has a groove or hollow in its centre, it is called complicated.  Plate IV. Fig. 6. *e*; those with few teeth are termed *articulate.*  Plate IV. fig. 1. and 12. and those with many teeth *multiarticulate.*  Plate IV. fig. 2. 3. 4, &c.  Plate I. fig. 6. and 8. *g g g g.*

*Primary teeth,* are those teeth in general situated in the centre of the hinge, and are for the most part broad, large, and distinct, often elevated; and in general are inserted in a cavity in the opposite valve.  They however differ very much in some shells, but may easily be distinguished.  Plate IV. fig. 1, 3, and 7. *a a a a a.*  These are also termed the Cardinal Teeth.

*Lateral Teeth,* Plate IV. fig. 10. are teeth which diverge from the umbo, and are in general long and flat, often double and divided by a groove or hollow.  Plate IV. fig. 2, 4, 6, and 7. *b b b b.*

*Double Teeth,* Plate IV. fig. 1. *c c.*

*Incurved Teeth* are those which are bent round, as in the single tooth of the Solen.  Plate IV. fig. 8. *f f.*

*Recurved Teeth,* are those which are bent backwards, as in the hinge of the Panopea.  Plate XVIII. fig. 9; and Spondylus, Plate II. fig. 8. *f f.*

*Middle Teeth,* Plate IV. fig. 4. *d d.*  These are also termed Cardinal Teeth.

*Numerous Teeth,* are those small upright teeth, set in rows, of which the hinges of all the species of the genus Arca are formed. Plate IV. fig. 10. *k k.*

*Cavity of the Hinge.*  The hollow depression in which the ligament of the Ostrea is situated, generally of a triangular form. Plate IV. fig. 11. *g.*

*Ligament* of the Hinge, or cartilage, is that flexible fibrous substance by which the valves are united, and the hinges kept in their proper places; generally situated under the beaks of the shell. Plate II. fig. 1, 3, and 4. *l l l;* Plate IV. fig. 3. *n.*

*Beak* is the extreme point of the summit of bivalves, which in many species turns spirally downwards, or to the one side, as in some species of Venus, &c.   From this circumstance it is seldom the highest part of the shell.   Plate II. fig. 5. *r r.*

*Seam.*   When the valves are closed, the line of separation between them is so called.   Plate II. fig. 6. *t t.*

*Umbo.*   That part situated immediately under the *beak.* Plate I., fig. 6. *w*; and Plate II. fig. 4. *w.*

*Ears.*   The processes on each side of the beak, in most species of that division of Ostrea, called pecten; some have one ear very large, and the other small; and some are scarcely observable on one side.   Plate IV. fig. 2. *h h.*

*Superior Ear.*   Plate IV. fig. 11. *h.*

*Inferior Ear.*   Do.   do.   *i.*

*Margin.*   The extreme edge of the whole shell, or the circumference of either valve, all round.   Plate I. fig. 4. *p;* and Plate II. fig. 1. *p.*

*Crenulated margin.*   That fine notched edge of shells, which unite into notches in the opposite valve, as genus Donax.   Plate IV. fig. 6. *m m.*

*Striæ* are fine thread-like lines, generally on the exterior surface of shells, and are sometimes both longitudinal and transverse. When the striæ of shells appear indistinct, as if worn out, it is termed *obsolete striæ.*   In some instances the insides of shells are striated; for example, the Fasciolaria tulipa.   The character of the striæ is often of much use in distinguishing species.   Plate II. fig. 2. *f.*

*Right Valve,* is that valve which, when viewed with the inside uppermost has the anterior slope pointing to the right hand. Plate I. fig. 8; and plate 4. fig. 5. and 6. *b.*

*Left Valve.*   The opposite of the above; the anterior slope points to the left hand, when viewed from the inside.   Plate IV. fig. 3, 6, 7, 9, &c.

*Length of the Shell* is taken from the ligament, or the beak, to the opposite margin.   For example, Mytilus: it is longer than it is broad, and the solens are broader than long.   Plate I. fig. 5. *u u.* and Plate II. fig. 4. *u u.*

*Breadth* is measured from the most extreme edge of the anterior and posterior slopes, being in a contrary direction from its length. Many shells are *broader than long*, such as most of the Myæ, Solenæ, Tellinæ, &c.; and the Mytilus, Ostrea, Pinna, &c. are in general longer than broad. Plate I. fig. 5. *v v*. Plate II. fig. 4. *v v*.

*Byssus*, or *beard*, is an appendage composed of filaments of a silky texture, by which some of the Bivalves fasten themselves to their beds, such as the Mytilus, Pinnæ, &c. Plate II. fig. 6. *s*.

## UNIVALVE.

The shells called univalve, or those composed of one part only, are far more numerous than the two preceding, both in genera and species; and it requires a considerable degree of attention to discriminate many of the *species*, as they run into each other so much; and they are divested of the strong and distinct character afforded by the teeth of bivalves; besides many of the species there are several varieties.

In the examination of shells of this order, the general contour or outline of the whole shell is the first particular to be attended to, as this leads to those distinctions necessary in the definition of simple, spiral, or turbinated shells, Univalves with a regular spire, and those without a regular spire. The genera of this order are formed principally from the shape of the aperture, taken in conjunction with the general shape of the shell; from the spire being lengthened or depressed, being with or without a canal, the length of the beak and its direction, together with the particular form of the outer lip: the colour of shells only serves as a specific distinction, and cannot in this respect, in all cases, be depended upon, although in others it is an unvarying test. The particular manner in which the spots are disposed, frequently characterises species.

*Apex*. The summit, tip, or highest part of the spire. Plate II. fig. 7, 8, 9. *A A A*.

*Base* is the opposite extremity from the apex, or tip of the spire. In shells with a beak it implies the tip of such beak; Plate II. fig. 11. *B*. In shells without a beak it is understood to be the lower part, as before-mentioned, opposite the apex; Plate II. fig. 8.

and 9. *B B*. In the Patella and some others, the base of the shell is that part on which it rests when it is laid on its mouth. In the Dentalium and Teredo it is the wider end.

*Body* of the shell is the first or lower whorl of the spire, in which the aperture is situated, and is in general longer than the remaining whorls. Plate II. fig. 10 and 12. *F F*. and Plate III. fig. 7 and 9. *F F*.

*Front* of the shell is that side where the aperture is situated. Plate II. fig. 7. *I*; and Plate III. fig. 8. *I*.

*Back* is the opposite side to that in which the aperture is placed or turned directly from the observer. Plate III. fig. 5. and 10. *G G*.

The *venter*, or belly, is the most prominent part of the lower whorl or body, generally situated in the vicinity of the lip over the aperture; and formed by the convexity of the aperture. It is in general only made use of in describing shells whose body is large in proportion to the size of the spire. Plate III. fig. 5 and 10. *H H*.

*Sides.* The extreme edges of the shell, when viewed either in front or from the back. Plate II. fig. 11. *K K K K K K K K*. Right side is, when the shell is viewed in front that side next the observer's left hand. Left side, the side with the aperture in it.

*Aperture*, or mouth, is that part of the lower whorl or body by which the animal protrudes itself. This is one of the principal generic distinctions of Univalve shells, and differs very much in shape; some apertures being rounded, others semilunar, angular, &c. Plate II. fig. 9 and 11. *C C*; and Plate III. fig. 1, 3, and 14. *C C C*. Some apertures have a canal at their base, and others are devoid of it. In various genera it extends the whole length of the shell, as in the Cypræa, and some of the Cones with depressed spires. This in several individuals is either entirely open, or is closed by an operculum or lid, which is usually affixed to the foot of the animal.

*Canal*, or gutter, is the inside of the elongations of the aperture, or both lips of the shell of those species with a beak in which it forms a concave channel or gutter, running from its

commencement in the aperture to the extremity or base, Plate
II. fig. 10 and 11. *Q Q.* Plate III. fig. 8. *Q.* Some species are
furnished with two canals, one situated at the junction of the outer
lip and body, as in the Murex.

*Beak*, is that lengthened process in which the canal is situate ;
it commences a little higher up, on the outside, than the insertion
of the canal in the inside, which is always distinctly marked by the
line of the aperture.   Plate II. fig 11. *p.*   This process is not so
conspicuous in some of the species of Voluta, but is more marked
in the genera Murex, Fusus, Pyrula, &c.

*Pillar*, or *columella*, is that process which runs through the
centre of the shell in the inside from the base to the apex in
most univalve shells, and appears to be the support of the spire :
and, indeed, seems to form that part of the shell : it is in general
grooved or folded ; but, as it is situated in the interior of the shell,
a minute description is unnecessary.   Plate II. fig. 10 and 12.
*M M M M M. ;* and plate III. fig. 9. *M M M.*   The internal
edge of its base is frequently described as having plaits, &c.

*Plaited Columella* are those folds, or plaits, which are the distinguishing characteristic of the Volutæ and other genera.   Plate
II. fig. 7. *z.*

*Pillar Lip* is a continuation of the glossy process with which
the aperture is lined, and expanded on the columella.   Plate III.
figures 7 and 8. *O O.*   This is termed the inner lip by some
authors.

*Outer Lip.*   The expansion, or continuation of the body of
the shell on the left margin of the aperture, and is also lined
with the glossy process of the aperture.   Plate II. fig. 7. *N* ; and
Plate III. fig. 8. *N N N.* The latter is an example of the alated
or winged shells.

*Operculum*, or lid.   This is only an appendage to the turbinated or spiral shells affixed to the foot of the animal, sometimes
of a testaceous, in others of a horny or cartilaginous substance.
It acts as a door or lid, and is calculated for the protection of the
animal, when it retires within its dwelling, from the intrusion of
its enemies, and adapted to the shape of the aperture, which it

closes nicely up : as exemplified in the operculum of the Turbo, and is of a hard stony appearance.   Plate III. fig. 4.

*Spire* consists of all the whorls of the shell, except the lower one, which, as before observed, is termed the body of the shell. Plate II. fig. 12. *D ;* and Plate III. figures 7 and 8. *D D.*

The spire is a prominent feature of the Univalve ; and upon its being elevated, depressed, &c. depends much of the generic and specific definition.   Adanson, in his 'Natural History of Senegal,' says that the external character of the spire varies according to the plane they turn upon, which, he observes, is either horizontal, cylindrical, conic, or ovoid.   At the same time, he admits that there are a great many intermediate forms which cannot properly be defined.

It must be remembered that many of the young shells have not the same number of wreaths as the adults ; from which it would appear, that the part of the animal nearest the apex never increases in size.   The number of wreaths cannot, at all times, be depended upon.   A full grown shell may, however, be known from the outer-lip, which has generally an unfinished appearance in young shells.   Indeed, in all the land and fresh water shells it is a distinct criterion, as they are never complete in the form of the outer-lip till full grown.

*Worl* is one of the wreaths or volutions of the shell.   Plate II. fig. 8. *L ;* and Plate III. fig. 10. *L.*

*Depressed Spire* is when the spire is very flat, as in the shells of the genus Planorbis, &c.   Pl. II. fig. 12. *d ;* and Pl. III. fig. 5. *s.*

A flat shell is figured in Plate III. fig. 14.

*Involuted Spire,* those shells which have their whorls, or wreaths, concealed in the inside of the first whorl or body, as in some of the Nautili and Cypræ.

*Suture of the Spire,* or whorls, is a fine spiral line, which separates the wreaths or whorls from each other ; it is sometimes crenulated, undulated, or sulcated, and not unfrequently elevated or projecting.   Plate II. *e. e.*

*Reversed,* or *Heterostrophe Spire,* is when the volutions of the spire revolve in the same manner as a common corkscrew, or when the aperture is placed downwards, the nature of the spire runs upwards from the right hand to the left, Plate III. fig. 13.

In some of the more depressed species of Helix, or Nautilus, great attention is requisite in order to ascertain which is really the upper side of the shell, for it is on that side the spiral turns are to be taken from the centre or apex; and, in most instances, this is to be determined by the oblique direction of the aperture to the under part, where the lip rarely extends so far as on the upper part. In fixed shells, such as Serpulæ, there is no difficulty, as the side which is sessile must be considered as the base or under part. Thus in the Serpula Lucida the fixed part is sometimes very small, and the mouth protends spirally upwards, in a contrary direction to the sun; and therefore must be considered a reversed or heterostrophe shell, the same as if the volutions nearest the mouth had turned laterally upon the centre or fixed ones. This shell, indeed, is most frequently found with regular lateral volutions; and though subject to great variety, with respect to contortions, it invariably turns the aperture one way.

In some species of Nautilus, however, there can be no rule to ascertain whether the shells are dextral or sinistral; for when the aperture is exactly central, the lip embraces the body equally, and the sides of the shell are similar. In others of that genus, as in N. Beccarii and Beccarii perversus, two shells, the principal distinction of which is the contrary turn of their volutions, it is easily determined by the convexity of the upper side, and, of course, the aperture being placed somewhat beneath.

*Chambers* are the cavities divided by partitions, at regular or irregular intervals; as in the Nautilus. Plate III. fig. 11, *w w w w w.*

In some of the Serpula there are also divisions, but they are not regular as in the Nautili; and besides, they differ from them in being devoid of a siphunculus or communication between the chambers, the animal forms a complete partition, and adds to its shell, which it would appear to be necessitated to do from its body growing too large for its abode.

Several of the Patellæ have chambers formed of laminous partitions, subspiral cells, or processes; these in general lie horizontally, and are quite open at one end, as in the Patella testudinaria, the Crepidula, and Calyptræa.

*Umbilicus* is in general a circular perforation in the base of the lower whorl, or body, of many univalve shells. This is common to most of the Trochi, in some species of which it penetrates from the base to the apex: widest at the base, and gradually tapering to the top. Plate III. fig. 1. *u.*

*Sub-umbilicated* shells are those which have the umbilicus covered in a greater or less degree by a thin process; which, in some, almost entirely closes the opening or mouth. This character is most commonly to be met with among species of Buccinum and Murex.

Shells which have no umbilicus are termed imperforate.

*Siphunculus* is that small round perforation which forms a communication between the chambers of the Nautili, and penetrates through the whole spire of the shell. Plate III. fig. 11. *v.*

*Varices* are transverse ribs which cross the whorls of shells in some species of Buccinum, Murex, and Tritonia, and exemplified in the Cassidaria. Varices are formed by the periodical growth of the shells, these being the margin of the outer lip, to which the animal has attached its periodical enlargements. In some species they have more the form of sutures than ribs; this is owing to the margin of the outer lip being but slightly developed.

*Ribs* are those longitudinal and transverse protuberances which are in many of the univalve shells. Plate III. fig. 12. *r r r r.*

*Teeth* of univalves, or tooth-shaped protuberances, are fine white laminæ, or ridges, running spirally backwards, in a parallel direction to each other; those on the exterior lip may, in most instances, be traced through the outside of the shell, and are nearly alike in length. Plate III. fig 13. *a.*

*Epidermis* is a skin, or cuticle, covering the exterior surface of shells, destined by nature to protect their surface from being injured. It is membranaceous, somewhat similar to the periosteum which covers the bones of animals. This substance is the production of the animal inhabiting the shell; it is uniformly observed in some species, and not at all in others. Shells with a rugged or uneven surface have almost always this epidermis. In some it is strong, laminated, velvety, fibrous, or rough, often beset with long hairs, and in others very thin, smooth, and pellucid, and admits the colours of the shell to shine through it. In some species it is so dusky that it entirely obscures the beautiful colouring of the shell beneath. Although many shells are very beautiful, even with this cuticle on them, they are much more so when it is removed ; but I would by no means advise the collector of shells to remove it, unless he may have several duplicates of the same species ; and then he may do it by way of variety. It is always preferable, however, to keep them in a state of nature.

A shell with epidermis is represented in Plate III. *X*; and the effect of the epidermis removed at *I*.

All other protuberances, furrows, &c. will be described at the end of this work, in a Glossary of Terms used in the Science.

## DESCRIPTION OF PLATE IV.

### HINGES OF BIVALVE SHELLS.

Fig. 1. Hinge of the Unio pictorum, *a* Primary tooth, *c c* double teeth.

Fig. 2. Hinge of the *Solen.* *b* Lateral teeth.

Fig. 3. Hinge of the Lucina radula, *a a* Primary teeth, *n* cartilage.

Fig. 4. Hinge of the *Cardium.* *b* Lateral tooth, *d d* middle teeth, *l l* spines.

Fig. 5. Hinge of the Lutraria.

Fig. 6. Inside of both valves of the *Donax trunculus.* *A* is the left valve, and *B* is the right valve, *b* lateral teeth, *b* primary complicated tooth, or cleft in the middle, *m m* crenulated margin.

Fig. 7. Hinge of the *Venus, a a* Primary teeth, *b* lateral tooth.

Fig. 8. Hinge of *Spondylus gæderopus, f f* incurved teeth.

Fig. 9. Hinge of Isocardia Cor.

Fig. 10. Hinge of the Pectunculus, *k k* numerous small teeth ; the distinguishing characteristic of the genus *Arca.*

Fig. 11. Hinge of the Pecten, *g* cavity of the hinge, *h* superior ear, *i* inferior ear.

Fig. 12. Hinge of *Anomia Ephippium.*

# CLASSIFICATION.

## CLASS I.

### ANNULATA.

#### FOUR FAMILIES.

Fam.
1. *Dorsalia.* Two genera.
   1. Arenicola. Species 1
   2 Siliquaria. " 5
2. *Maldania.* Two genera.
   1. Clymene. Species 1
   2. Dentalium. " 14
3. *Amphitritæa.* Four genera.
   1. Pectinaria. Species 2
   2. Sabellaria. " 2
   3. Terebella. " 4
   4. Amphitrite. " 7
4. *Serpulacea.* Five genera.
   1. Spirorbis. Species 6
   2. Serpula. " 26
   3. Vermilia. " 9
   4. Galeolaria. " 2
   5. Magilus. " 2

## CLASS II.

### CIRRHIPEDA.

#### ONE FAMILY.

1. *Cirrhipeda.* Ten genera.
   1. Tubicinella. Species 1
   2. Cor onja. " 4
   3. Balanus. " 29
   4. Acusta. " 4
   5. Caeusia. " 3
   6. Pryrgoma. " 1
   7. Anatifera. " 6
   8. Pollicipes. " 5
   9. Cineras. " 1
   10. Otion. " 2

## CLASS III.

### CONCHIFERA.

#### TWENTY FAMILIES.

Fam.
1. *Tubicola.* Six genera.
   1. Aspergillum. Species 4
   2. Clavagella. " 1
   3. Fistulana. " 4
   4. Septaria. " 2
   5. Teredina. " 2
   6. Teredo. " 3
2. *Pholadaria.* Two genera.
   1. Pholas. Species 13
   2. Gastrochæna. " 3
3. *Solenea.* Four genera.
   1. Solen. Species 19
   2. Panopea. " 1
   3. Solecurtus. " 3
   4. Glycimeris. " 2
4. *Myaria.* Two genera.
   1. Mya. Species 4
   2. Anatina. " 10
5. *Mactracea.* Seven genera.
   1. Lutraria. Species 11
   2. Mactra. " 34
   3. Crassatella. " 11
   4. Erycina. " 1
   4. Ungulina. " 2
   6. Solemya. " 2
   7. Amphidesma. " 36
6. *Corbulacea.* Two genera.
   1. Corbula. Species 13
   2. Pandora. " 4
7. *Lithophaga.* Three genera.
   1. Saxicava. Species 5
   2. Petricola. " 13
   3. Venerirupis. " 8

Fam.

8. *Nymphacea.* Ten genera.
  1. Sanguinolaria. Species 5
  2. Psammobia. " 18
  3. Psammotea. " 8
  4. Tellina. " 55
  5. Tellinides. " 1
  6. Corbis. " 2
  7. Lucina. " 22
  8. Donax. " 28
  9. Capsa. " 3
  10. Crassina. " 1

9. *Conchacea.* Seven genera.
  1. Cyprina. Species 9
  2. Cytherea. " 89
  3. Venus. " 99
  4. Veniricardia. " 15
  5. Cyclas. " 11
  6. Cyrena. " 11
  7. Galathea. " 1

10. *Cardiacea.* Five genera.
  1. Cardium. Species 64
  2. Cardita. " 25
  3. Cypricardia. " 7
  4. Hiatella. " 2
  5. Isocardia. " 5

11. *Arcacea.* Four genera.
  1. Arca. Species 46
  2. Cucullæa. " 2
  3. Pectunculus. " 31
  4. Nucula. " 44

12. *Trigonacea.* Two genera.
  1. Trigonia. Species 16
  2. Castalia. " 1

13. *Naiadea.* Four genera.
  1. Unio. Species 167
  2 Hyria. " 2
  3. Anodonta. " 49
  4. Iridina. " 6

14. *Chamacea.* Three genera.
  1. Diceras. Species 1
  2. Chama. " 25
  3. Etheria. " 5

15. *Tridacnea.* Two genera.
  1. Tridacna. Species 7
  2. Hippopus. " 1

Fam.

16. *Mytilacea.* Three genera.
  1. Mytilus. Species 36
  2. Modiola. " 25
  3. Pinna. " 15

17. *Mallacea.* Five genera.
  1. Crenatula. Species 7
  2. Perna. " 12
  3. Malleus. " 6
  4. Avicula. " 14
  5. Meleagrina. " 2

18. *Pectinea.* Seven genera.
  1. Pedum. Species 1
  2. Lima. " 17
  3. Pecten. " 157
  4. Plagiostoma. " 10
  5. Plicatula. " 5
  6. Spondylus. " 26
  7. Podopsis. " 2

19. *Ostracea.* Six genera.
  1. Ostrea. Species 81
  2. Gryphea. " 1
  3. Vulsella. " 7
  4. Placuna. " 5
  5. Anomia. " 9
  6. Crania. " 1

20. *Brachiopoda.* Three gen.
  1. Orbicula. Species 3
  2. Terebratula. " 49
  3. Lingula. " 1

---

# CLASS IV.

## MOLLUSCA.

TWENTY-THREE FAMILIES.

1. *Pteropoda.* Six genera.
  4. Hyalea. Species 2
  2. Clio. " 2
  3. Cleodora. " 2
  4. Limacina. " 1
  5. Cymbulia. " 1
  6. Pneumodermon " 1

Fam.
2. *Phyllidiacea.* Six genera.
  1. Phyllidia.    Species 3
  2. Chitonellus.    "   2
  3. Chiton.    "   60
  4. Patella.    "   45
  5. Umbrella.    "   2
  6. Pleurobranchus. "   2
3. *Calyptracea.* Seven gen.
  1. Parmophorus. Species 5
  2. Emarginula.    "   5
  3. Fissurella.    "   20
  4. Pileopsis.    "   5
  5. Calyptrea.    "   8
  6. Crepidula.    "   7
  7. Ancylus.    "   3
4. *Bullacea.* Three genera.
  1. Acera.    Species 1
  2. Bullæa.    "   2
  3. Bulla.    "   14
5. *Aplysiacea.* Two genera.
  1. Dolabella.    Species 2
  2. Aplysia.    "   37
6. *Limacina.* Five genera.
  1. Limax.    Species 5
  2. Vitrina.    "   3
  3. Testacella.    "   2
  4. Parmacella.    "   2
  5. Onchidium.    "   2
7. *Colimacea.* Eleven genera.
  1. Helix.    Species 168
  2. Carocolla.    "   22
  3. Achatina.    "   22
  4. Anostoma.    "   3
  5. Helicina.    "   19
  6. Pupa.    "   33
  7. Clausilia.    "   15
  8. Bulimus.    "   61
  9. Succinea.    "   7
  10. Auricula.    "   16
  11. Cyclostoma.    "   35
8. *Lymnacea.* Three genera.
  1. Lymnea.    Species 17
  2. Physa.    "   6
  3. Planorbis.    "   14

Fam.
9. *Melaniana.* Three genera.
  1. Melania.    Species 29
  2. Pirena.    "   5
  3. Melanopsis.    "   3
10. *Peristomiana.* Three gen.
  1. Valvata.    Species 2
  2. Paludina.    "   19
  3. Ampularia.    "   13
11. *Neritacea.* Four genera.
  1. Neritina.    Species 28
  2. Nerita.    "   20
  3. Navicella.    "   4
  4. Natica.    "   36
12. *Ianthinea.* One genus.
  1. Ianthina.    Species 3
13. *Macrostomiana.* Four gen.
  1. Sigaretus.    Species 4
  2. Stomatella.    "   5
  3. Stomatia.    "   2
  4. Haliotis.    "   19
14. *Plicacea.* Two genera.
  1. Tornatella.    Species 6
  2. Pyramidella.    "   6
15. *Scalarina.* Three genera.
  1. Scalaria.    Species 14
  2. Vermetus.    "   2
  3. Delphinula.    "   11
16. *Turbinacea.* Eight gen.
  1. Solarium.    Species 15
  2. Trochus.    "   107
  3. Monodonta.    "   34
  4. Turbo.    "   43
  5. Planaxis.    "   4
  6. Phasianella.    "   12
  7. Turritella.    "   51
  8. Rotella.    "   7
17. *Canalifera.* Eleven gen.
  1. Cerithium.    Species 47
  2. Pleurotoma.    "   59
  3. Turbinella.    "   23
  4. Cancellaria.    "   68
  5. Fasciolaria.    "   15
  6. Fusus.    "   79
  7. Pyrula.    "   35

Fam.
8. Struthiolaria.   Species 2
9. Ranella.         "   19
10. Murex.        "   75
11. Triton.         "   34
18. *Alata.*   Three genera.
   1. Rostellaria.   Species 7
   2. Pterocera.     "   12
   3. Strombus.      "   37
19. *Purpurifera.*   Eleven gen.
   1. Cassidaria.   Species 12
   2. Cassis.        "   33
   3. Ricinula.      "    9
   4. Purpura.      "   55
   5. Monoceros.    "    5
   6. Concholepas.   "    1
   7. Harpa.        "    8
   8. Dolium.       "    7
   9. Buccinum.     "   72
   10. Eburna.      "    5
   11. Terebra.      "   24

Fam.
20. *Columellaria.*   Five genera.
   1. Columbella.   Species 14
   2. Mitra.        "   80
   3. Voluta.       "   44
   4. Marginellæ.   "   33
   5. Volvaria.     "    5
21. *Convoluta.*   Six genera.
   1. Cypræa.   Species 118
   2. Ovula.       "   12
   3. Terebellum.   "    3
   4. Ancillaria.    "    9
   5. Oliva.       "   68
   6. Conus.      "   181
22. *Nautilacea.*   Two genera.
   1. Spirula.   Species 1
   2. Nautilus.    "   17
23. *Heteropoda.*   Two genera.
   1. Argonauta.   Species 3
   2. Carinaria.    "   3

---

The American species are designated by a *.

# CONCHOLOGY.

---

## CLASS I.

### ANNULATA.

Animal soft, elongated, vermiform, naked or inhabiting a tube, which it never entirely quits; the body furnished either with segments or transverse wrinkles; often without a head, eyes or antennæ; without articulated feet, but most of them having in their place bristly retractile knobs, disposed in lateral rows: mouth subterminal, either simple, orbicular, with lips, or in the form of a proboscis; often with jaws, a knotted longitudinal medulla, and nerves for sensation and motion; the blood red, circulating by means of arteries and veins: respiration by external or internal branchiæ, which are sometimes imperceptible. *Four Families.*

### FAMILY I.

#### DORSALIA.  Two Genera.

##### 1. Genus *Arenicola.*

*Animal.* The gills, or respiratory organs dorsal, or disposed lengthways on the body.

*Shell.* Supposed to be tubular.  One species.

A.  Piscatorium.

##### 2. Genus *Siliquaria.*  Pl. V.

*Animal.* See Arenicola.

*Shell* very thin, conical, tubular, involuted in a spiral manner, loosely and irregularly; aperture circular, sharp edges, interrupted in the middle by a notch, extending like a slit through the greater portion of its length, and stopping abruptly at some distance from the summit.   Inhabits the Indian Seas.   Five species.

|                      |                      |
|----------------------|----------------------|
| Siliquaria Anguina.  | Siliquaria Lævigata. |
| S. Muricata.         | S. Lactæa.           |
|          S. Rugosa.  |                      |

## FAMILY II.

### Maldania.   Two Genera.

#### 1. Genus *Clymene*.

*Animal*.   Respiratory organs not determined, supposed to be at the posterior part of the body.

*Shell*.   Tube thin and slender, open at both ends, encrusted externally with sand and fragments of shells.   One species.

C. Amphistoma.

#### 2. Genus *Dentalium*.   Pl. V.

*Animal*.   Body elongated, conical, sub-vermiform, enveloped in a fistular mantle as far as the anterior third, and ending in a bourrelet pierced in its middle by an orifice with fringed edges; foot altogether anterior, proboscidiform, terminated by a conical appendage, contained in a kind of cup with festooned edges; head distinct, oval, with a terminal mouth in the middle of a digitated lip; a pair of lateral jaws, formed each of two little oval shells garnished with points.

*Shell*.   Tubular, regular, symmetrical, slightly curved longitudinally, tapering gradually to the rear, and opening in a round orifice at each end.   Inhabits the British seas.   Fourteen species.

|                         |                        |
|-------------------------|------------------------|
| Dentalium elephantinum. | Dentalium octoganum.   |
| D. aprinum.             | D. novemcostatum.      |
| D. fasciatum.           | D. dentale.            |
| D. entale.              | D. nigrum.             |
| D. tarentinum.          | D. politum.            |
| D. corneum.             | D. eburneum.           |
| D. lutea.               | D. Swainsonicnse.      |

## FAMILY III.

### AMPHITRITÆA.  Four Genera.

#### 1. Genus *Pectinaria.*  Pl. V.

*Animal.*  Respiratory organs in general known, and disposed at or near the anterior part of the body; not separated or covered by an operculum.

*Shell.*  A membranous or papyraceous tube in the form of a reversed cone; unfixed; exterior covered with sandy adhesions. Two species.

Pectinaria belgica.          Pectinaria capensis.

#### 2. Genus *Sabellaria.*  Pl. V.

*Animal.*  But slightly differing from the Pectinaria.

*Shell.*  Composed of fragments and particles of marine substances, adhering to a tubular membrane; some are detached, others fixed; tubes cellular at the base; orifice expanded.  Two species.

Sabellaria alveolata.          Sabellaria crassissima.

#### 3. Genus *Terebella.*  Pl. V.

*Animal.*  Body tubicular, elongated, cylindrically depressed, attenuated posteriorly; a row of nodulous and setiferous papillæ on each side; numerous filiform, twisted tentacula surrounding the mouth.

*Shell.*  An elongated cylindrical and membranous tube, attenuated and pointed at the base; with sandy adhesions.  Inhabits the coast of New Holland.  Four species.

Terebella conchilega.          Terebella cristata.
T. ventricosa.                 T. vermicuta.

#### 4. Genus *Amphitrite.*  Pl. V.

*Animal.*  Body tubicular, elongated, cylindrical, attenuated behind with many annulated segments.

*Shell.*  An elongated cylindrical tube growing thinner towards the base, of a tough membranous texture, and generally without adhesions.  Mediterranean sea.  Seven species.

Amphitrite ventilabra.          Amphitrite vesiculosa.

A. penicilla.

A. magnifica.

A. volutacornis.

A. infundibula.

A. minima.

## FAMILY IV.

Serpulacea. Five Genera.

### 1. Genus *Spirorbis*. Pl. V.

*Animal.* Gills or respiratory organs separated or covered by an operculum.

*Shell.* A testaceous tube turned spirally on a horizontal plane, the lower portion of which is attached to marine substances, generally fuci; opening of the tube terminal, rounded or angular. Found on Algæ on the British coast. Six species.

Spirorbis nautiloidis.

S. spirilla.

S. tricostalis.

Spirorbis bicarinata.

S. carinata.

S. lamellosa.

### 2. Genus *Serpula*. Pl. V.

*Animal.* Body tubular, elongated, depressed and attenuated behind; segments numerous and narrow; small bundles of awl-shaped bristles in a single row on each side.

*Shell.* A solid calcareous tube, brown, purple, yellow, tawny, pink, white, or tinged with green. The shells are irregularly twisted, in clusters, and affixed to other substances. Inhabits the coast of Britain. Twenty-six species.

Serpula vermicularis.

S. fascicularis.

S. intestina.

S. contortuplicata.

S. plicaria.

S. glomerata.

S. decussata.

S. protensa.

S. infundibula.

S. annulata.

S. cereola.

S. filograna.

S. vermicella.

Serpula filaria.

S. pellucida.

S. intorta.

S. cristata.

S. spirulæa.

S. quadrangularis.

S. minima.

S. echinata.

S. sulcata.

S. costalis.

S. dentifera.

S. sipho.

S. arenaria.

### 3. Genus *Vermilia*. Pl. V.

*Animal.* Body tubicular, elongated and attenuated towards the posterior part, and provided superiorly with a simple testaceous orbicular operculum.

*Shell.* A testaceous cylindrical tube, narrowed in the rear, twisted, and adhering by the side to marine substances. Inhabits the British coast. Nine species.

| | |
|---|---|
| Vermilia rostrata. | Vermilia subcrenata. |
| V. triquetra. | V. plicifera. |
| V. bicarinata. | V. scabra. |
| V. eruca. | V. tæniata. |

V. plicata.

### 4. Genus *Galeolaria*. Pl. V.

*Animal.* Distinguished from the vermilia by a very peculiar operculum.

*Shell.* In groups, testaceous, cylindrical, subangular, wavy, adhering by the base, and open at the summit; aperture orbicular, terminated on the side by a spatular tongue; operculum orbicular, squamose, and consisting of from five to nine testaceous parts or valves. Inhabits the Indian seas. Two species.

Galeolaria cæspitosa.          Galeolaria elongata.

### 5. Genus *Magilus*. Pl. V.

*Animal.* Unknown.

*Shell.* Usually found imbedded in a species of Madrepore. Base bent into a spiral form, oval, with four contiguous, convex volutions (the last of which is the largest), and prolonged into a straight waved tube, convex above, carinated beneath. Inhabits the sea at the Isle of France. Two species.

Magilus antiquus.          Magilus muricatus.

# CLASS II.

## CIRRHIPEDA.

*Animal.* Soft, without head or eyes, testaceous, body fixed as if reversed, inarticulated, furnished with a mantle, having above tentacular arms, with curled tufts multiarticulated, mouth beneath, not projecting, dentated transverse jaws disposed in pairs. Number of arms, unequal and varying, disposed in rows, each composed of two rows of curled tufts of bristles; fringed; a corneous skin supported by a pedicle. Medulla longitudinal and knotted; gills external, sometimes concealed; circulation by heart and vessels. One Family.

### FAMILY.

CIRRHIPEDA. ·Ten Genera.
1. Genus *Tubicinella.* Pl. V.

*Animal.* Body inclosed in a shell, with small setaceous and unnequal cirri.

*Shell.* Univalve, operculated, tubular, erect, a little attenuated towards the base, bound with annular transverc ribs, truncated at both ends, open at the summit, and closed at the base with a membrane. Operculum with four obtuse valves. South American seas. One species.

Tubicinella valanarum.

2. Genus *Coronula.* Pl. V.

*Animal.* Body seated, enveloped in a shell with small setaceous and cirrous arms.

*Shell.* Sessile, apparently indivisible, suborbicular, conoidal or blunt, conical, the extremities truncated, the sides very thick, the inside hollowed into radiating cells. Operculum composed of four obtuse valves. Inhabits the north seas. Four species.

Coronula diadema.　　　　Coronula valænaris.
C. testudinaria.　　　　　C. pulchra.

### 3. Genus *Balanus*. Pl. V.

*Animal.* Body sessile, inclosed in an operculated shell; branchiæ numerous, placed in two rows, unequal, articulated, cilliated; each composed of two cirri, supported by a peduncle, and exsertile; mouth with four transverse dentated jaws, with four hairy palpi-like appendages.

*Shell.* Formed of six distinct coronary valves, one dorsal, one ventral, and two pairs of laterals, with a calcareous support; operculum forming a sort of pyramid, by four articulated pieces in the aperture of the shell. Inhabits the Frith of Forth. Twenty-nine species.

| | |
|---|---|
| Balanus angulosus. | Balanus tintinabulus. |
| B. negrescens. | B. calycularis. |
| B. roseus. | B. miser. |
| B. amphimorphus. | B. subimbricatus. |
| B. crispatus. | B. palmatus. |
| B. stalaciferus. | B. dupluconus. |
| B. patellaris. | B. semiplicatus. |
| B. perforatus. | B. lævis. |
| B. rugosus. | B. punctatus. |
| B. latus. | B. sulcatus. |
| B. plicatus. | B. cylindraceus. |
| B. galeatus. | B. ovularis. |
| B. spinosus. | B. radiatus. |
| B. placianus. | B. fistulosus. |

B. Lyonsii.

### 4. Genus *Acasta.* Pl. V.

*Animal.* Body without a peduncle, and inclosed in a multi-valve shell, found in sponge or marine bodies, mouth and tentacula placed in the apex, or upper part of the body.

*Shell.* Patella-shaped, sub-conically oval, formed of six lateral unequal valves forming the base, which being convex prevents the shell from standing by itself in an erect position, when detached from the substance which envelopes it. Inhabits the British seas. Four species.

Acasta montaguii.      Acasta glans.
A. sulcata.      A. tubulosa.

## 5. Genus *Creusia*. Pl. V.

*Animal.* Body, subglobular, inclosed in an operculated shell; having three or four pairs of tentacular arms: mouth at the anterior part of the body.

*Shell.* Sessile, fixed, orbicular, conical, consisting of four united unequal valves; attached to madrepore and other marine substances, they are almost microspopic, and found only in the seas of hot countries. Inhabits the China seas. Three species.

Creusia stromia.      Creusia spinulosa.
C. verruca.

## 6. Genus *Pyrgoma*. Pl. V.

*Animal.* As above.

*Shell.* Sessile, univalve, rather globular, ventricose, convex above; apex perforated; aperture small, elliptical, operculum quadrivalve. Inhabits the Indian seas. One species.

Pyrgonia cancellata.

## 7. Genus *Anatifera*. Pl. V.

*Animal.* Body covered with a shell, supported by a long tubular tendinous peduncle; with long, numerous, and unequal tentacular arms, which are articulated and ciliated, and emanating from the summit on one side.

*Shell.* Compressed on the sides, with five flat valves, the valves contiguous and unequal; the lower lateral ones the largest: the whole of them united and kept together by means of their membranes. Inhabits the British seas. Six species.

Anatifera lævis.      Anatifera dentata.
A. villosa.      A. striata.
A. vitrea.      A. Aculeata.

### 8. Genus *Pollicipes*. Pl. V.

*Animal.* Body covered by a shell, and supported on a tabular, tendinous, scaly peduncle; with many tentacular arms.

*Shell.* Compressed at the sides, multivalve, contiguous, unequal in number, with numerous small valves situated at the base; peduncle covered with embricated scales, lower ones rounded and turned upward. Inhabits the European seas. Five species.

Pollicipes cornucopia.       Pollicipes mitella.

P. scalpellum.                P. peronii.

P. homii.

### 9. Genus *Cineras*. Pl. V.

*Animal.* Body pedunculated, and encased in a membranous tunic, which is swollen above, with an opening below the summit, from which protrude many ciliated articulated arms.

*Shell.* composed of five testaceous oblong valves, two at the sides of the aperture and three on the back, not covering the whole of the body; supported by a peduncle of a greenish color, with several longitudinal stripes. Inhabits the British coast, One species.

Cineras vittata.

### 10. Genus *Otion*. Pl. V.

*Animal.* Body pedunculated, enveloped in a membranous tunic, which is ventricose above; two horn-like tubes, directed backwards, truncated, and open at their points, and situated in the apex of the tunic; having a lateral opening, with many articulated and ciliated arms.

*Shell.* Composed of two testaceous valves, attached near the lateral opening, the centre aperture admitting the animal's tentaculæ, the singular form of which prevents its being blended with the genus cineras without a further examination of its structure. Inhabits the North seas. Two species.

Otion Cuvieri.                Otion Blainvillii.

# CLASS III.

## CONCHIFERA.

*Animals.* Soft, inarticulated, always fixed in a bivalve shell, without head or eyes, having the mouth naked, concealed, and without any hard parts ; a large mantle enveloping the whole of the body, forming two laminiform lobes, the edges detached or sometimes united in front.   Gills or respiratory organs external, situated on each side between the body and the mantle ; circulation simple, the heart with one ventricle ; some few ganglions of the different nerves, but no knotted medullary cord.

*Shell.*   Always bivalve, enveloping the animal entirely or partially, sometimes free, sometimes affixed ; the valves most frequently united on one side by a hinge or ligament, sometimes attached to the shell, are testaceous accessory pieces.   Twenty families.

## FAMILY I.

### Tubicola.   Six Genera.

#### 1. Genus *Aspergillum.*   Pl. V.

*Animal.*   Entirely unknown.

*Shell.* Oval, somewhat elongated, striated longitudinally, conic, club-shaped, open at its attenuated extremity, and terminated at the other by a convex disk, pierced by a number of small perforations, and encircled by a dilated margin of papyraceous tubes, resembling a plaited ruff, smaller extremity always open.   This is a well known, but rare shell, found in sandy places in low water in the Indian ocean.   Four species.

Aspergillum Javanum.     Aspergillum Novæ Zælandiæ.
A. vaginiferum.          A. agglutinans.

#### 2. Genus *Clavagella.*   Pl. VI.

*Animal.*   Unknown.

*Shell.* A tubular sheath, testaceous, attenuated, and open before ;

terminating posteriorly in an oval, sub-compressed club, rough-ened by spiniform tubes. Inhabits the Indian seas. One species. Clavagella aperta.

### 3. Genus *Fistulana*. Pl. VI.

*Animal*. Provided with two protuberant calcareous tubes, cover-ing parts of its body at the open end of the tube, each of which is terminated with from five to eight cup-shaped calcareous, or corneous appendages. It inhabits the sand, and perforates wood, stones, and sometimes shells.

*Shell*. Lamarck asserts that the tube and shell of this genus are quite distinct. They have the shell free and detached within the sheath, and neither of the valves fixed into the partition of the tube, which is most generally testaceous, closed, and retort-shaped at the posterior extremity. Inhabits the Indian seas. Four species.

| | |
|---|---|
| Fistulana clava. | Fistulana gregata. |
| F. corniformis. | F. lagenula. |

### 4. Genus *Septaria*. Pl. VI.

*Animal*. Unknown.

*Shell*. A very long testaceous tube, gradually attenuated to its upper end, and divided internally by vaulted divisions seldom complete, the extremity of which is terminated by two slender tubes without interior partitions. Specimens of this genus have been found five feet long. Found in sand on the shores of the Indian sea. Two species.

Septaria arenaria.        Septaria maculata.

### 5. Genus *Teredina*. Pl. VI.

A fossil genus; consisting of a testaceous cylindrical sheath, the posterior extremity closed, and exhibiting the two valves of the shell it encloses; the anterior end open. Two fossil species.

### 6. Genus *Teredo*. Pl. VI.

*Animal*. Body very much elongated, vermiform : mantle very fine, tubular, opening only at front and below for the issue of a teat-shaped foot; mouth small ; very short, distinct tubes ; the inferior or respiratory one somewhat larger than the superior ; labial appendages short and striated ; branchiæ very long, narrow, united, and prolonged throughout the extent of the tubular cavity of the mantle ; only one large contractile muscle between the valves ; at the point of junction of the mantle and tubes is a muscular ring, in which is implanted a pair of corneo-calcareous appendages.

*Shell.* Thick, solid, very short or annular, open before and behind ; valves equal, equilateral, angular and trenchant before, only touching each other by the opposite edges ; no hinge ; a considerable spoonlike cavity ; only one feeble muscular impression, Tube more or less distinct from the substance in which the animal lives, cylindrical, straight or winding, and closing with age at the bucal extremity so as to envelope the animal and its shell; at the other end it is always open, and divided internally into two syphons by a partition in the middle. Inhabits the European seas in timber. Three species.

Teredo navalis.      Teredo palmulata.      Teredo gigantea.

## FAMILY II.

### Pholidaria.   Two Genera.

#### 1. Genus *Pholas.*   Pl. VI.

*Animal.* Without a tubular sheath, projecting anteriorly into two united tubes, frequently surrounded by a common skin, and the posterior extremity provided with a short muscular foot, flattened at its extremity.

*Shell.* Multivalve, equivalve, transverse gaping at both ends, with various accessory pieces either on the hinge or below it. Inhabits Indian seas and American shores.   Thirteen species.

| | |
|---|---|
| Pholas dactyla. | Pholas silicula. |
| P. orientalis. | P. costata.* |
| P. candida. | P. callosa. |
| P. dactiloides. | P. clavata. |
| P. papyracea. | P. ovum. |
| P. tuberculata. | P. lancellata.* |
| P. crispata. | |

2. Genus *Gastrochæna.*  Pl. VI.

*Animal.*  Unknown.

*Shell.*  Equivalve, somewhat cuneiform with a very large oval and oblique aperture anteriorly ; posterior extremity nearly closed ; hinge linear ; marginal and without teeth.  Three species.

Gastrochæna cuneiformis.     Gastrochæna mytiloides.

G. modiolina.

## FAMILY III.

### SOLENIDA.  Four genera.

#### 1. Genus *Solen.*  Pl. VI.

*Animal.*  Body cylindroid, much elongated ; the mantle in form of a canal open at both ends, closed in the rest of its extent by a thick epidermis which surrounds it ; a cylindroid anterior foot.

*Shell.*  Equivalve, extremely inequilateral, the summits very small, and entirely at the commencement of the dorsal line ; one or two teeth in the hinge.    Inhabits the seas of America and Europe.    Nineteen species.

| | |
|---|---|
| Solen vaginus. | Solen vaginoides. |
| S. corneus. | S. siliqua. |
| S. ensis. | S. cultellus. |
| S. pygmæus. | S. planus. |
| S. ambiguus. | S. minutus. |
| S. dombeii. | S. constrictus. |
| S. javanicus. | S. coarctatus. |
| S. caribæus. | S. rostratus. |
| S. antiquatus. | S. violaceus. |

S. giganteus.

#### 2. Genus *Panopæa.*  Pl. VI.

*Animal.*  Unknown.

*Shell.*  Regular oval, elongated, gaping at both ends, equivalve, inequilateral ; summit little marked and anterodorsal ; hinge complete ; similen formed by a conical primary tooth, before a short, compressed, ascending callosity, ligament exterior, attached to the

5

callosity; two muscular impressions. Inhabits the Mediterranean sea. One species.

Panopæa aldrovandi.

### 3. Genus *Solecurtus*. Pl. VI.

*Animal.* Unknown.

*Shell.* Oval, elongated, equivalve, subequilateral, with edges nearly straight and parallel, the extremities equally rounded, and, as it were, truncated; summits but little marked; hinge without teeth, or formed by some rudimentary primary teeth, ligament projecting, affixed to thickened callosities; two distinct rounded muscular impressions. Mediterranean sea. Three species.

Solecurtus radiatus. Solecurtus strigilatus.

S. legumen.

### 4. Genus *Glycimeris*. Pl. VI.

*Animal.* Unknown.

*Shell.* Covered with epidermis, slightly irregular, elongated, gaping at both ends, equivalve, exceedingly inequilateral; summits little marked; hinge toothless; a longitudinal callosity. Ligament exterior, affixed to very projecting callosites on the shortest side of the shell; two distinct muscular impressions. Inhabits the north seas. Two species.

Glycimeris margaritacea. Glycimeris siliqua.

## FAMILY IV.

### MYARIA. Two genera.

### 1. Genus *Mya*. Pl. VI.

*Animal.* Subcylindrical, enveloped in a mantle pierced only with one interior and inferior hole for the passage of a very small and conical foot; the tubes very considerable, and completely united; a tolerably large mouth, oval, and with simple lips; very small labial appendages; branchial laminæ inconsiderable; the external very short, the internal united with that of the opposite side.

*Shell.* Surrounded with a thick epidermis, which is prolonged upon the tubes and the edges of the mantle of the animal; tolerably solid, with fine trenchant edges ; the summits very little marked ; hinge dissimilar ; one or two oblique cardinal folds, divergent, behind a horizontal spoon-shaped hollow upon the left valve, corresponding with a hollow ; horizontal and cardinal in the right valve ; two distinct muscular impressions. Inhabits the British coast. Four species.

| | |
|---|---|
| Mya truncata. | Mya erodona. |
| M. arenaria. | M. solenimyalis. |

### 2. Genus *Anatina.* Pl. VI.

*Animal.* Unknown.

*Shell.* Transverse, subequivalve, gaping at both valves, or in one only ; no cardinal teeth ; one broad primary tooth in both valves, projecting interiorly ; a lateral plate running obliquely under the primary teeth. Sometimes there is a fissure extending from the apex, giving the appearance of a second plate or rib Inhabits the British seas. Ten species.

| | |
|---|---|
| Anatina laterna. | Anatina trapezoides. |
| A. truncata. | A. rugosa. |
| A. subrostrata. | A. imperfecta. |
| A. longirostris. | A. myalis. |
| A. globulosa. | A. rupicola. |

### FAMILY V.

MACTRACEA. Seven genera.

### 1. Genus *Lutraria.* Pl. VI.

*Animal.* Body oval, much compressed, or subcylindrical ; the mantle enclosed only in the half of its inferior side : foot small and projecting but little beyond the abdominal mass, tubes long, distinct or united.

*Shell.* Oval or elongated, regular, equivalve, more or less inequilateral, sometimes but slightly gaping ; edges always simple and trenchant ; summits feebly marked ; hinge subsimilar, formed by two very small divergent cardinal teeth ; two very distinct muscular impressions united by a palleal impression profoundly sinuous to the rear. Inhabits the seas of Europe. Eleven species.

Lutraria solenoides.      Lutraria elliptica.
L. rugosa.      L. papyracea.
L. compressa.      L. Plicatella.
L. piperata.      L. crassiplica.
L. tellinoides.      L. complanata.
L. candida.

## 2. Genus *Mactra*.

*Animal.* Body oval and pretty thick; edges of the mantle thick, smooth, or without tentacular papillæ, augmented behind by two indistinct tubes; mouth small and oval; labial appendages narrow; branchial laminæ very small, and united in their length among themselves and with those of the opposite side; foot oval, trenchant, very long.

*Shell.* The Mactra has a peculiar hinge distinguishing it from all other genera. It is triangular, with a curved or angular compressed tooth on each valve, with a small oblique cavity on each side, to which is attached the ligament. Two lateral teeth, one near the primary tooth and one near the ligament. The shape of the shell is subtriangular or oblong; exterior smooth, striated, or ribbed transversely; two muscular impressions united by a narrow marginal tongue. Inhabits the British coasts. Thirty-four species.

Mactra gigantea.      Mactra helvacea.
M. spengleri.      M. grandis.
M. striatella.      M. stultorum.
M. carinata.      M. maculosa.
M. straminea.      M. ovalina.
M. Australis.      M. alba.
M. violacea.      M. solida.
M. fasciata.      M. castanea.
M. turgida.      M. rufa.
M. plicataria.      M. squalida.
M. rufescens.      M. brasiliana.
M. maculata.      M. donacina.
M. subplicata.      M. depressa.
M. triangularis.      M. lilacea.

M. lactea.          M. trigonella.
M. abbreviata.      M. deltoides.
M. crassatella.     M. alata.

### 3. Genus *Crassatella*.

*Animal.* Unknown.

*Shell.* Close, suborbicular or transverse, striated longitudinally, denticulated, regular, equivalve, inequilateral, summits well marked, and turned to the front: primary teeth somewhat divergent with a hollow at the side ; no lateral teeth nor obsolete ones; ligament internal and inserted into a pit in the hinge. It is easily known from the Mactra and Lutraria by the valves fitting exactly. The living species of this genus only exist in the seas of Australasia, while in a fossil state we find at least seven species in France. Eleven species.

Crassatella kingicola.      Crassatella subradiata.
C. donacina.                C. contraria.
C. sulcata.                 C. cuneata.
C. rostrata.                C. Erycinæa.
C. glabrata.                C. cycladea.
              C. striata.

### 4. Genus *Erycina*.

*Animal.* Unknown.

*Shell.* Somewhat longer than high, subtrigonal, regular equivalved, inequilateral, gaping but little or not at all ; sumits well marked and a little inclined to the front; hinge subsimilar; two unequal cardinal teeth converging to the summit; two oblong, compressed, short, and inserted lateral teeth; ligament internal and situated in a pit. Owing to the equivocal character of this genus it is somewhat difficult to judge of the hinge. Inhabits the Indian Ocean. One species.

                Erycina cardioides.

### 5. Genus *Ungulina*.

*Animal.* Unknown.

*Shell.* Vertical or sublongitudinal, a little irregular, not gaping,

5*

equivalve, subequilateral, with summits a little marked; hinge dorsal, formed by a cardinal tooth; two long muscular impressions, one short primary cleft tooth in each valve, with an oblong groove divided in the middle of the margin, ligament internal, inserted in a pit. Two species.

Ungulina oblonga.       Ungulina transversa.

## 6. Genus *Solemya*.

*Animal.* Unknown.

*Shell.* Covered with a thick epidermis, enclosing it entirely except at the extremities, regular, somewhat thick, oval, elongated, straight and parallel edges, also rounded at its two extremities, valves equal, very inequilateral; the anterior side much longer than the posterior; summits feebly marked; hinge subsimilar, formed by a cardinal tooth, dilated, compressed, and a little reflexed above; subexterior ligament inserted upon the tooth, and nearly at the posterior extremity of the shell; two small, rounded, widely separated muscular impressions, without any visible abdominal impression. Two species.

Solemya australis.       Solemya mediterranea.

## 7. Genus *Amphidesma*.

*Animal.* Very imperfectly known.

*Shell.* Transverse, inequilateral, somewhat rounded or suboval; sides slightly gaping; hinge with one or two cardinal teeth, and a narrow groove for the internal ligament; ligament double, the external one short, the internal one fixed in the internal grooves. The two ligaments distinguish this genus from all other bivalves. Inhabits the West Indian seas. Thirty-six species.

| | |
|---|---|
| Amphidesma variegatum. | Amphidesma Tenuii. |
| A. donacillum. | A. purpurescens. |
| A. lacteum. | A. nucleolum. |
| A. corneum. | A. physioides. |
| A. albellum. | A. pulchrum. |
| A. flexuosum. | A. pallidum. |
| A. prismaticum. | A. formosum. |
| A. phaseolinum. | A. roseum. |
| A. corbuloides, | A. ellipticum. |

A. glabrellum.

A. lucinale.

A. Boysii.

A. lenticulare.

A. cancellatum.

A. reticulatum.

A. duplicatum.

A. læve.

A. prismaticum.

A. subtruncatum.

A. solidum.

A. cordiforme.

A. rupium.

A. lamellosum.

A. crenulatum.

A. punctatum.

A. multicostatum.

A. siculum.

## FAMILY VI.

### Corbulacea. Two genera.

### 1. Genus *Corbula.*

*Animal.* Unknown.

*Shell.* Tolerably solid, regular, inequivalve, inequilateral with a conical, flexed, ascending, primary tooth in each valve; a cavity at the side; no lateral teeth; ligament interior, placed in the cavities; two neighbouring muscular impressions. Inhabits the British seas. Nine species. Four fossil.

Corbula australis.

C. sulcata.

C. erythrodon.

C. ovalina.

Corbula taitensis.

C. nucleus.

C. impressa.

C. porcina.

C. semen.

### 2. Genus *Pandora.*

*Animal.* Body much compressed, somewhat elongated, in form of a furrow, in consequence of the union of the edges of the mantle, and its continuation with the tubes, which are united and short; foot small, thickest in front, and issuing through a tolerably large cleft in the mantle.

*Shell.* Regular, white, elongated, much compressed, inequivalved, inequilateral; right or upper valve quite flat, with a fold; summits feebly marked; hinge anomalous, formed by a transverse cardinal tooth on the right; valve entering a corresponding cavity in the left; ligament internal, oblique, triangular, inserted in a somewhat deep pit, with edges a little projecting on each valve; two round muscular impressions. Inhabits the Mediterranean and British seas. Two living species, and two fossils, according to Defrance.

Pandora rostrata. Pandora obtusa.

## FAMILY VII.

### Lithophagi. Three genera.

#### 1. Genus *Saxicava*.

*Animal.* Long, subcylindrical, the mantle closed in all parts, prolonged behind by two long tubes, thick and close together externally, pierced interiorly and in front with a round orifice, for the passage of a very small foot; mouth very large; labial appendages small; branchial laminæ free, the external pair much shorter than the internal.

*Shell.* Thick, with an epidermis, a little irregular, elongated, subcylindrical, obtuse at both ends; summits feebly marked; hinge toothless, or with a very small rudimentary tooth; ligament external, somewhat inflated; two round muscular impressions, distinct, and several others, irregular. Inhabits the British seas, and cavities which they bore in rocks or wood. Five species.

Saxicava Rugosa. Saxicava pholadis.
S. gallicana. S. australis.
S. veneriformis.

#### 2. Genus *Petricola*.

*Animal.* Unknown.

*Shell.* Subtrigonal, more or less irregular, transverse, inequilateral; upper side narrowed and a little gaping; lower side rounded; hinge with two teeth in each valve, or in one valve only. Inhabits the Australian seas, boring into wood and rocks. Thirteen species.

Petricola lamellosa. Petricola rocellaria.
P. Ochrolenca. P. exilis.
P. Semilamellata. P. ruperella.

P. lucinalis.

P. striata.

P. costellata.

P. chamoides.

P. pholadiformis.

P. labagella.

P. linquatula.

### 3. Genus *Venerirupis.*

*Animal.* Unknown, but probably resembling the Venus.

*Shell.* Transverse, inequilateral, posterior side short, the anterior gaping slightly. Hinge with two teeth on the right valve, three on the left, and sometimes three on both—these are small, near together and parallel. Ligament exterior. Inhabits the British seas, boring into rocks and clay. Eight species.

Venerirupis perforans

V. nuclea.

V. Ira.

V. carditoides.

Venerirupis exotica.

V. distans.

V. crenata.

V. alata.

## FAMILY VIII.

### Nymphacea. Ten genera.

This family is divided into N. Solenaria and N. Tellinaria, from their resemblance to the Solen and Tellina.

### N. Solenaria. Three genera.

### 1. Genus *Sanguinolaria.*

*Animal.* Unknown.

*Shell.* Oval, compressed, a little elongated, gaping but little, equivalve, subequilateral, rounded at both extremities; no mark of posterior keel; summits feebly marked; hinge formed by one or two contiguous cardinal teeth upon each valve; ligament projecting; two round muscular impressions, distant and joined by a narrow palleal impression strongly sinuous behind. Inhabits the sea at Jamaica. Five species.

Sanguinolaria occidens.

S. rosea.

Sanguinolaria livida.

S. rugosa.

S. alba.

## 2. Genus *Psammobia*.

*Animal.* Unknown.

*Shell.* Transverse, oblong-ovate, or elliptical, flattened, slightly gaping at one side ; summits projecting ; hinge formed by two primary teeth in the left valve, and one in the opposite one. Inhabits the European seas. Eighteen species.

| | |
|---|---|
| Psammobia virgata. | Psammobia alba. |
| P. ferroensis. | P. cayennensis. |
| P. vespertina. | P. lævigata. |
| P. florida, | P. tellinella. |
| P. muculosa. | P. pulchella. |
| P. cærulescens. | P. aurantia. |
| P. elongata. | P. fragilis. |
| P. flavicans. | P. livida. |
| P. sqamosa. | P. galathea. |

## 3. Genus *Psammotæa*.

*Animal.* Unknown.

*Shell.* Of the same form as the Psammobia, but differing in the number of teeth, the left valve of the Psammotæa having only one tooth ; and sometimes one valve is without teeth, while the other has two ; ligament exterior, attached to callosities at the hinge, and without an irregular plait. Inhabits the Australian seas. Seven species. One fossil species.

| | |
|---|---|
| Psammotæa violacea. | Psammotæa candida. |
| P. zonalis. | P. tarentina. |
| P. pellucida. | P. donacina.  · |
| P. serotina. | |

## N. TELLIRINA. Seven Genera.

The two last of these genera have no lateral teeth, the rest have one or two.

## 4. Genus *Tellina*.

*Animal.* Body triangular, much compressed ; the free edge of the mantle furnished with a row of tentacular largest and longest in the rear ; foot very large, compressed and pointed to the front ; buccal appendages nearly as large as the bronchial laminæ, of which the external pair are much smaller than the internal; the anterior contractile muscle larger than the other; tubes very distinct.

*Shell.* Of a somewhat variable form, generally striated longitudinally and much compressed, equivalved, more or less inequilateral; the anterior side almost always longer and more rounded than the posterior, which constantly presents a flexuous fold, at least at its inferior edge; summits feebly marked; hinge similar, one or two cardinal teeth; two lateral teeth, far apart with a pit at their base in each valve; ligament posterior, large; round muscular impressions. The finest species of this beautiful shell are found in the pearl fisheries of Ceylon. Fifty-five species.

| | |
|---|---|
| Tellina unimaculata. | Tellina margaritina. |
| T. virgata. | T. strigosa. |
| T. semizonalis. | T. planata. |
| T. staurella. | T. punicea. |
| T. lutirostra. | T. depressa. |
| T. rostrata. | T. pulchella. |
| T. spengleri. | T. fabula. |
| T. radiata. | T. tenuis. |
| T. crucigera. | T. sulphurea. |
| T. elliptica. | T. cornuta. |
| T. albinella. | T. irrisa. |
| T. rosea. | T. levigata. |
| T. foliacea. | T. linquafelis. |
| T. operculata. | T. rugosa. |
| T. chloraleuca. | T. lacunosa. |
| T. remies. | T. gargadia. |
| T. sulcata. | T. pristis. |
| T. crassa. | T. gigas. |
| T. exilis. | T. scalaris. |
| T. donacina. | T. psamotella. |
| T. nitida. | T. scobinata. |
| T. striatula. | T. brasiliana. |
| T. decussata. | T. umbonella. |
| T. obliqua. | T. deltoidalis. |
| T. nymphalis. | T. multangula. |

| | |
|---|---|
| T. solidula. | T. capsoides. |
| T. polygona. | T. serradiata. |
| T. ostracea. | T. vimaculata. |

### 5. Genus *Tellinides*.

*Animal.* As above.

*Shell.* Equilateral, transverse, somewhat elongated, nearly without the flexuous plait; two divergent cardinal teeth of which the anterior is but little distant from the summit. Inhabits the Bay of Naples. One species.

Tellinides Timorensis.

### 6. Genus *Corbis*.

*Animal.* Differing slightly from the Lucina.

*Shell.* Equivalve, transverse, without any irregular fold on the anterior margin, having the beaks flexed inward and opposite; two cardinal teeth; two lateral, the posterior of which is nearest the hinge; muscular impressions simple, ligament external. Inhabits the Indian Ocean. Two species.

| | |
|---|---|
| Corbis fimbriata. | Corbis maculata. |

### 7. Genus *Lucina*.

*Animal.* Very imperfectly known.

*Shell.* Inequilateral, suborbicular, beaks small, pointed, and oblique; two divergent cardinal teeth, one of which is bifid, and which vary or disappear with age; two lateral teeth sometimes obsolete, the posterior approaches nearest to the cardinal teeth; two muscular impressions far apart, the posterior in shape of a band, sometimes very long; ligament external. Inhabits the British seas. Twenty-two species.

| | |
|---|---|
| Lucina jamaicensis. | Lucina divaricata. |
| L. edentula. | L. scabra. |
| L. radula. | L. sinuata. |
| L. lactea. | L. lutea. |
| L. undata. | L. globularis. |
| L. circinaria. | L. digitalis. |
| L. columbella. | L. Pecten. |

| | |
|---|---|
| L. Pennsylvanica. | L. reticulata. |
| L. mutabilis. | L. carnaria. |
| L. squamosa. | L. concentrica. |
| L. Peruviana. | L. fimbriata. |

### 8. Genus *Donax.*

*Animal.* As in Tellina.

*Shell.* Transverse, inequilateral, equivalve; anterior side short and obtuse; two primary teeth in one or both valves; one or two lateral teeth varying in distance; two round muscular impressions; ligament, external, short, and inserted at the posterior impression. Inhabits the seas of Europe. Twenty-eight species.

| | |
|---|---|
| Donax pubescens. | Donax columbella. |
| D. cuneata. | D. australis. |
| D. radians. | D. bicolar. |
| D. abbreviata. | D. merois. |
| D. ringens. | D. scripta. |
| D. Cayennensis. | D. trunculata. |
| D. denticulata. | D. flabagella. |
| D. cinatina. | D. Martiniænsis. |
| D. cardioides. | D. triquetra. |
| D. scorta. | D. rugosa. |
| D. compressa. | D. elongata. |
| D. deltoides. | D. granosa. |
| D. veneriformis. | D. epidermia. |
| D. vittata. | D. minima. |

### 9. Genus *Capsa.*

*Animal.* As above.

*Shell.* Transverse, equivalve, valves approximate and close; three primary teeth in the right valve, and a single bifid tooth in the left, inserted into a cavity in the opposite one; no lateral teeth; ligament external and on the short side, as in Donax. Inhabits the Indian Ocean. Three species.

| | |
|---|---|
| Capsa levigata. | Capsa Braziliensis. |

C. Donaoides.

### 10. Genus *Crassina.*

*Animal.* As above.

*Shell.* Distinguished from the Venus by having only two teeth on each valve, and from the crasatella by the position of the ligament; solid, sub-orbicular, thick, hinge with two strong diverging primary teeth in the right valve, and two unequal ones on the other; ligament external. Inhabits the Scottish and Devonshire coasts. One species.

Crassina Danmoniensis.

## FAMILY IX.

Conchacea.   Seven Genera.

This family is divided into *Conchæ marinæ,* and *Conchæ fluviatiles.*

Conchæ Marinæ.   Four Genera.

### 1. *Cyprina.*

*Animal.* Thick, oval, foot compressed, falciform, geniculated; mantle closed behind, and pierced by two oval apertures with cirrous edges; no veritable tubes.

*Shell.* With epidermis; thick, regular, substriated longitudinally, subcordiform, equivalved, inequilateral; summits strongly flexed to the front and often contiguous; hinge thick, subsimilar, formed by three slightly converging cardinal teeth, and by a posterior lateral tooth, sometimes obsolete; ligament very thick; muscular impressions distant, subcircular, and united by a narrow marginal band. Inhabits the Atlantic ocean and British seas. Two living species. Seven fossil.

Cyprina tennistria.          Cyprina Icelandica.

### 2. Genus *Cytherea.*

*Animal.* Oval or round, generally but little compressed; edges of the mantle undulous, and garnished with tentacular cirrhi in one row; foot considerable, compressed, trenchant, in other respects diversiform; tubes tolerably elongated, and most usually united; mouth small; labial appendages quite small; branchiæ wide, short, free, or not united either with one another, or with those of the opposite side.

*Shell.* Solid, equivalve, regular, inequilateral; summits equal, reflexed, and slightly projecting; four primary teeth on one valve, of which three are divergent, and approximating at the base, and one remote—this circumstance easily distinguishing it from the Venus. On the other valve are three primary divergent teeth with a distant cavity parallel with the edge. Inhabits the British and Mediterranean seas. Eighty living species. Nine fossil.

| | |
|---|---|
| Cytherea petechialis. | Cytherea tigrina. |
| C. morphina. | C. pulicaris. |
| C. Castanea. | C. numulina. |
| C. casta. | C. abbreviata. |
| C. lusoria. | C. pectinata. |
| C. graphica. | C. flexuosa. |
| C. impudica. | C. ranella. |
| C. purpurata. | C. lunularis. |
| C. zonaria. | C. divaricata. |
| C. corbicula. | C. lunaris. |
| C. meretrix. | C. placunella. |
| C. tripla. | C. cygnus. |
| C. erycina. | C. juvenilis. |
| C. impar. | C. gigantea. |
| C. Guiniensis. | C. Venetiana. |
| C. pectoralis. | C. lilacina. |
| C. Arabica. | C. rufa. |
| C. florida. | C. erycinella. |
| C. immaculata. | C. Dione. |
| C. Chione. | C. planatella. |
| C. hepatica. | C. trimaculata. |
| C. citrina. | C. nitidula. |
| C. lactea. | C. pellucida. |
| C. lata. | C. maculata. |
| C. lineta. | C. lucinalis. |
| C. trigonella. | C. albina. |
| C. prostrata. | C. exoleta. |

.C. Hebræa.                    C. mactroides.
C. tigerina.                   C. concentrica.
C. ornata.                     C. sulcatina,
C. umbonella.                  C. interrupta.
C. castrensis.                 C. punctata.
C. picta.                      C. undatina.
C. scripta.                    C. gibbia.
C. mixta.                      C. macrodon.
C muscaria.                    C. testudinalis.
C. plicatina.                  C. rugifera.
C. dentaria.                   C. aspergata.
C. nodulosa.                   C. squamosa.
C. cuneata.                    C. cardilla.

### 3. Genus *Venus*.

*Animal.* As above.

*Shell.* Solid, thick, regular, perfectly equivalved and close, more or less inequilateral; summits well marked and inclined to the front; hinge subsimilar; the middle cardinal tooth forked, or three cardinal teeth more or less contiguous and convergent towards the summits; ligament thick, often arcuated, convex, exterior; two distant muscular impressions; cordiform depressions beneath the beaks. Inhabits the British seas. Ninety living species. Nine fossil.

Venus reticulata.             Venus floridella.
V. rugosa.                    V. aphrodina.
V. corbis.                    V. pulchella.
V. crebiscula.                V. aphrodinoides.
V. discina.                   V. tristis.
V. cancellata.                V. flammea.
V. marica.                    V. puerpera.
V. sulcaria.                  V. verrucosa.
V. cardivides.                V. pygmæa.
V. texturata.                 V. casina.
V. elliptica.                 V. crenulata.
V. rariflamma.                V. plicata.
V. mercenaria.                V. granulata.

V. pullastra.

V. gallina.

V. truncata.

V. pectinula.

V. anomala.

V. lamellata.

V. exilis.

V. rufa.

V. Scotica.

V. hiantina.

V. virginea.

V. corugata.

V. ovulæa.

V. papilionacea.

V. callipyga.

V. punctifera.

V. nebulosa.

V. literata.

V. carneola.

V. petalina.

V. cornularis.

V. adspersa.

V. opima.

V. turgida.

V. flammiculata.

V. strigosa.

V. Perronii.

V. elegantina.

V. undulosa.

V. vermiculosa.

V. vulvina.

V. pectorina.

V. cingulata.

V. textilis.

V. grisea.

V. geographica.

V. Dombeii.

V. decussata.

V. lagopus.

V. glandina.

V. gallinula.

V. retifera.

V. sulcata.

V. galactites

V. exalbida.

V. scalarina.

V. dorsata.

V. aurea.

V. crassisulca

V. marmorata

V. Malabarica.

V. laterisulca.

V. subrostrata.

V. phaseolina.

V. florida.

V. bicolor.

V. catenifera.

V. sinuosa.

V. rimularis.

V. ovata.

V. pumila.

V. inquinata.

#### 4. Genus *Venericardia*.

*Animal.* Nearly as above.

*Shell.* Suborbicular, inequilateral, equivalve, sides having usually longitudinally rayed ribs ; hinge with two oblique cardinal

6*

teeth in each valve, turned in the same direction.  Five living
species.  Ten fossil species.

| | |
|---|---|
| Venericardia Australis. | Venericardia flammea. |
| V. imbricata. | V. Tankervillii. |

V. crassicosta.

CONCHÆ FLUVIATILES.   Three Genera.

### 5. Genus *Cyclas.*

*Animal.*  Body oval, thick ; edges of the mantle simple ; tubes
short and united ; foot wide, compressed at base, and terminated
by a sort of leg or appendage.

*Shell.*  With an epidermis, oval, or sub-orbicular, regular, equivalved, inequilateral ; summits obtuse, contiguous or turned
anteriorly ; hinge similar, complex, formed by a slightly variable
number of cardinal teeth, and by two separated lateral teeth with
a pit at the base ; ligament exterior, posterior, and inflated ; two
distant muscular impressions, united by a faintly marked abdominal band, and without posterior excavation.   Eleven species.

| | |
|---|---|
| Cyclas cornea. | Cyclas rivicola. |
| C. obliqua. | C. lacustris. |
| C. obtusalis. | C. calyculata. |
| C. Australis. | C. fontinalis. |
| C. striatina. | C. sulcata |

*C.  Sarratogea.

### 6. Genus *Cyrena.*

*Animal.*  As above.

*Shell.*  Rounded and trigonal, ventricose, inequilateral ; hinge
with three teeth on each valve ; two lateral teeth, one of which is
near the primary ones ; ligament exterior, situated on the largest
side.   The apices are always eroded or carious in shells of this
genus.   Inhabits the rivers of China.   Ten living species.   One
fossil.

| | |
|---|---|
| Cyrena orientalis. | Cyrena trigonella. |
| C. depressa. | C. cor. |

| | |
|---|---|
| C. fuscata. | C. Caroliniensis. |
| C. violacea. | C. fluminea. |
| C. Ceylonica. | C. Bengalensis. |

### 7. Genus *Galathea.*

*Animal.* As above.

*Shell.* Equivalve, subtrigonal, covered with a greenish epidermis; the surface beneath is white, with several violet streaks radiating from the summit to the margin; two furrowed cardinal teeth upon one valve, three upon the other, the middle one being largest and callous; muscular impressions double and lateral. Inhabits the rivers of Ceylon. One species.

Galathea radiata.


## FAMILY X.

### CARDIACEA. Five Genera.

#### 1. Genus *Cardium.*

*Animal.* Body somewhat inflated; mantle edged with tentacular cirrhi in all its inferior part; tubes united, of moderate size, and provided with cirrhi at the extremity; mouth transverse, very wide, with moderate labial appendages; foot very large, cylindrical, somewhat inclined anteriorly; branchiæ thick, rather small, especially the external laminæ: the internal united in all their extent.

*Shell.* Inflated, equivalve, sub-cordiform (when viewed anteriorly, usually costated from the apex to the circumference); summits very evident, but slightly flexed to the front; hinge complex, similar, formed of two oblique, conical cardinal teeth, and of two distant lateral teeth, upon each valve; ligament dorsal, posterior and very short. Inhabits the European seas. Fifty living species. Fourteen fossil.

| | |
|---|---|
| Cardium indicum. | Cardium costatum. |
| C. asiaticum. | C. ringens. |
| C. fimbriatum. | C. tennicostatum. |
| C. aculeatum. | C. pseudolima. |

| | |
|---|---|
| C. tuberculatum. | C. erinaceum. |
| C. apertum. | C. basilianum. |
| C. bullatum. | C. papyraceum. |
| C. echinatum. | C. ciliare. |
| C. biradiatum. | C. levigatum. |
| C. pectinatum. | C. eolicum. |
| C. isocardium. | C. elongatum. |
| C. angulatum. | C. rugosum. |
| C. serratum. | C. unedo. |
| C. medinum. | C. fragum. |
| C. tumotiferum. | C. lineatum. |
| C. retusum. | C. edule. |
| C. rusticum. | C. latum. |
| C. Greendlandicum. | C. exigunum. |
| C. crenulatum. | C. rosenum. |
| C. minotum. | C. hemicardium. |
| C. scobinatum. | C. junoniæ. |
| C. cardissum. | C. muricatum. |
| C. inversum. | C. marmoreum. |
| C. ventricosum. | C. sulcatum. |
| C. obtusum. | C. cifidium. |

### 2. Genus *Cardita.*

*Animal.* Body suborbicular, terminated superiorly by a sort of hook; mantle but little open; foot terminated at its extremity by a part much narrower than the base; superior lobes of the branchiæ very short.

*Shell.* Thick, solid, equivalve, more or less inequilateral; summit dorsal, always much flexed anteriorly; hinge similar, formed by two oblique teeth, one short, cardinal or apicial, the other post-apicial, long, lamellous and arcuated; ligament elongated, subexterior and inserted, two very distinct muscular impressions, united by a palleal band, narrow and semicircular. Inhabits the Mediterranean. Twenty-one living species. Four fossil.

| | |
|---|---|
| Cardita Ajar. | Cardita sulcata. |
| C. squamosa. | C. turgida. |
| C. crassicosta. | C. phrenetica. |

C. calyculata.

C. nodulosa.

C. trepezia.

C. depressa.

C. sinuata.

C. citrina.

Corbularis.

C. rufescens.

C. subaspera.

C. intermedia.

C. bicolor.

C. concamerata.

C. aviculina.

C. sublevigata.

C. lithophagella.

### 3. Genus *Cypricardia*.

*Animal.* As above.

*Shell.* Obliquely elongated, equivalve, inequilateral; valves striated, not ribbed; distinguished from the Cardita by having three teeth beneath the apices, and a callous lengthened tooth or ridge. Inhabits the coast of Guinea. Four living species. Three fossil.

Cypricardia angulata.

C. Guinaica.

Cypricardia coralliophaga.

C. rostrata.

### 4. Genus *Hiatella*.

*Animal.* Unknown.

*Shell.* Thin, elongated, subrhomboidal, equivalve, very inequilateral, gaping at its inferior edge, and at its posterior extremity; summit very anterior, and much flexed to the front; hinge formed of a single tooth upon one valve corresponding to an emargination in the opposite valve, or of a small tooth with a cardinal pit upon each valve; ligament exterior and dorsal. Inhabits the British seas. Two species.

Hiatella Arctica.

Hiatella biaperta.

### 5. Genus *Isocardia*.

*Animal.* Body very thick: edges of the mantle finely papillaceous, separated inferiorly, and united behind by a transverse band, pierced with two orifices surrounded with radiating papillæ; foot small, compressed, trenchant.

*Shell.* Free, regular, inflated, equivalve, very inequilateral, with diverging summits, strongly flexed anteriorly and outwardly,

in a commencing spiral, hinge dorsal, long, similar, formed of
two flat cardinal teeth and one lamellous behind the ligament;
ligament dorsal, exterior, diverging anteriorly towards the summit; muscular impressions very distant and small. Inhabits the
Mediterranean and British seas. Four living species. One fossil.

| | |
|---|---|
| Isocardia Moltikana. | Isocardia cor. |
| I. retusum, | I. semisulcata. |

## FAMILY XI.

### ARCACEA. Four Genera.

#### 1. Genus *Arca*.

*Animal.* Body thick, slightly variable in form; abdomen provided with a pedunculated foot, compressed, fit for adhesion, and
cleft throughout its extent; mantle supplied with a simple row
of cirrhi and slightly prolonged posteriorly; buccal tentacula
very small and very thin.

*Shell.* Somewhat diversiform, but most usually elongated and
more or less oblique at the posterior extremity, often very inequilateral; summits more or less distant and little flexed to the front;
hinge anomalous, straight, or a little flexed, long and formed by a
line of short vertical teeth, decreasing from the extremities to the
centre; ligament exterior, wide, nearly as much before as behind
the summit; two muscular impressions united by a band or
palleal impression, not very distinct. Inhabits the American and
British seas. Thirty-seven living species. Nine fossil.

| | |
|---|---|
| Arca semitorta. | Arca inequivalvis. |
| A. tetragona. | A. tortuosa. |
| A sinuata. | A. Noæ. |
| A. cardissa. | A. umbonata. |
| A. retusa. | A. avellana. |
| A. ovata. | A. ventricosa. |
| A. scapha. | A. sulcata. |
| A. fusca. | A. Helbingii. |
| A. Domingensis. | A. barbata. |
| A. trapezina. | A. Magellanica. |

A. pisolina.

A. callifera.

A. bisulcata.

A. senilis.

A. auriculata.

A. Cayennensis.

A. antiquata.

A. Braziliana.

A. lactea.

A. cancellaria.

A. irudina.

A. rhombea.

A. corbicula.

A. Indica.

A. granosa.

A. squamosa.

A. pistachia.

## 2. Genus *Cucullæa.*

*Animal.* As above.

*Shell.* Trapeziform, inequilateral, equivalve, heart-shaped; beaks far apart, separated by the angular groove of the ligament, which is altogether external; hinge linear, straight, with small transverse teeth, having at its extremity from two to five parallel ribs; valves minutely striated longitudinally; margins crenulated. The Cucullæa is distinguished from the Arca by the muscular impression, to one side of which is an auriform testaceous appendage; the shell also is more trapeziform. Inhabits the Indian ocean. One living species. One fossil.

Cucullæa auriculifera.

## 3. Genus *Pectunculus.*

*Animal.* Body round, more or less compressed; mantle without cirrhi or tubes; foot securiform, cleft at its inferior anterior edge; buccal appendages linear.

*Shell.* Orbicular, equivalve, subequilateral; summit nearly vertical, and more or less distant; hinge formed upon each valve, of a numerous series of small teeth disposed in a curved line, sometimes interrupted beneath the summit; ligament as in Arca, but usually much narrower. Inhabits the British and Mediterranean seas. Twenty-two living species. Nine fossil.

Pectunculus pilosus.

P. marmoratus.

P. angulatus.

P. palleus.

P. zonalis.

Pectunculus pennaceus.

P. castaneus.

P. striatularis.

P. pectinatus.

P. rubeus.

P. glycimeris.

P. undulatus.

P. scriptus.

P. stellatus.

P. violacescens.

P. aggregatus.

P. pectiniformis.

P. nummarius.

P. radiaus.

P. vitreus.

P. inscriptus.

P. cinerosus.

## 4. Genus *Nucula.*

*Animal.* Body subtriquetral; mantle open in its inferior half only, with whole edges, denticulated throughout the extent of the back, without posterior prolongation; foot very large, thin at the root, enlarged into a wide oval disk, the edges of which are furnished with tentacular digitations; anterior buccal appendages, pretty long, pointed, stiff, and applied one against the other like jaws; the posterior ones also stiff and vertical.

*Shell.* More or less thick, subtriquetral, equivalved, inequilat eral, with summits contiguous and inclined anteriorly; hinge similar, formed by a numerous series of very sharp teeth, pectinated and arranged in a line interrupted under the summit; ligament internal, short, inserted in a little oblique pit in each valve; two muscular impressions. Inhabits the British seas. Forty living species. Four fossil.

Nucula lanceolata.

N. pella.

N. obliqua.

N. elongata.

N. tellinoides.

N. crenifera.

N. arctica.

N. curvirostra.

N. glacialis.

N. fluviatilis.

N. minuta.

N. para.

N. Mauritiania.

N. limatula.

N. lævis.

Nucula rostrata.

N. Nicobarica.

N. Margaritacea.

N. costellata.

N. gibbosa.

N. eburnea.

N. polita.

N. nasuta.

N. fabula.

N. Elenensis.

N. cuneata.

N. striata.

N. rugulosa.

N. nitida.

N. tenuis.

N. concentrica.

N. convexa.

N. decussata.

N. Pisum.

N. exijua.

N. carinifera.

N. squamosa.

N. torta.

N. gigantea.

N. plicarla.


## FAMILY XII.

### TRIGONACEA.  Two genera.

#### 1. Genus *Trigonia.*

*Animal.*  Entirely unknown.

*Shell.*  Subtrigonal or suborbicular, thick, regular, equivalve, inequilateral; summits but slightly prominent, little flexed, anterodorsal; hinge complex, dorsal, dissimilar; two thick oblong teeth joined angularly under the summit, strongly furrowed upon the right valve, penetrating into two excavations of the same form, also furrowed, in the left valve; ligament postapicial; two distinct muscular impressions, not united by a band.  Inhabits the Australian seas.  One living species.  Fifteen fossil species.

Trigonia pectinata.

#### 2. Genus *Castalia.*

*Animal.*  Body large, slightly compresssed, or moderately thick, more or less oval; mantle with thick edges, simple or broken, open in all its circumference except towards the back; a kind of small, incomplete tube, furnished with two rows of somewhat elongated cirrhi for the respiratory cavity; flamelliform and trenchant.

*Shell.*  Subtrigonal, equivalve, inequilateral; umbones eroded, covered with epidermis, and flexed anteriorly; hinge with two lamellar teeth transversly striated, one distant, posterior and shortened, the other anterior, long, and lateral; ligament exterior. Habitation unknown.  One species.

Castalia ambigua.

7

## FAMILY XIII.

NAIADEA. Four genera.

### 1. Genus *Unio*.

*Animal.* See *Castalia*.

*Shell.* Usually very thick, nacred within, covered with epidermis, corroded at the summits, which are dorsal and subanterior ; dorsal hinge formed by a double precardinal tooth, more or less compressed, irregularly dentated on the left valve, and simple on the right, together with a long lamellous tooth under the ligament ; ligament external, dorsal and postapicial ; two muscular impressions, well marked, besides those of the retractile muscles. The species of this genus grow more numerous daily ; they are found in all countries, but particularly in North America. One hundred and sixty-seven defined species. Numerous fossil.

| | |
|---|---|
| Unio Batavus. | Unio crassidens. |
| U. crassissimus. | U. obliquus. |
| U. elongatus. | U. plicatus. |
| U. litoralis. | U. purpuratus. |
| U. pictorum. | U. radiatus. |
| U. platyrhnchus. | U. rectus. |
| U. marginalis. | U. retusus. |
| U. Leaii. | U. rotundatus. |
| U. tigris. | U. Australis. |
| U. Egyptiacus. | U. Nova Hollandica. |
| U. Niloticus. | |

The following species are American.

| Unio Bengalensis. | *Lea.* | U. lamellatus. | *Lea.* |
|---|---|---|---|
| U. bilineatus. | ,, | U. Morchisonianus. | ,, |
| U. cæruleus. | ,, | U. olivarus. | ,, |
| U. corrugatus. | ,, | U. ponderosus. | ,, |
| U. Corrianus. | ,, | U. divaricatus. | ,, |
| U. Graianus. | ,, | U. acutissimus. | ,, |
| U. alatus. | ,, | U. fabalis. | ,, |
| U. andontoides. | ,, | U. Fisherianus. | ,, |

| | | | |
|---|---|---|---|
| U. augustatus. | *Lea.* | U. folliculatus. | *Lea.* |
| U. apiculatus. | ,, | U. fulvus. | ,, |
| U. arcæformis. | ,, | U. gibber. | ,, |
| U. arctior. | ,, | U. glaber. | ,, |
| U. asperrimus. | ,, | U. glans. | ,, |
| U. asper. | ,, | U. globosus. | ,, |
| U. Blandingianus. | ,, | U. graniferus. | ,, |
| U. Barnesianus. | ,, | U. Griffithianus. | ,, |
| U. brevidens. | ,, | U. Haysianus. | ,, |
| U. camelus. | ,, | U. heterodon. | ,, |
| U. capsæformis. | ,, | U. Hildrethianus. | ,, |
| U. carbonarius. | ,, | U. Hopetonensis. | ,, |
| U. castanus. | ,, | U. Hydianus. | ,, |
| U. claibornensis. | ,, | U. inflatus. | ,, |
| U. circulus. | ,, | U. interruptus. | ,, |
| U. occineus. | ,, | U. iris. | ,, |
| U. compressus. | ,, | U. irroratus. | ,, |
| U. complanatus. | ,, | U. Jayensis. | ,, |
| U. confertus. | ,, | U. jegunus. | ,, |
| U. congaræus. | ,, | U. Katherinæ. | ,, |
| U. contradens. | ,, | U. Kirklandianus. | ,, |
| U. Cooperianus. | ,, | U. lævissimus. | ,, |
| U. creperus. | ,, | U. lacrymosus. | ,, |
| U. cuprinus. | ,, | U. lancolatus. | ,, |
| U. Cumberlandicus. | ,, | U. Lecontianus. | ,, |
| U. decisus. | ,, | U. lens. | ,, |
| U. dolabriformis. | ,, | U. lugubris. | ,, |
| U. donaciformis. | ,, | U. luteolus. | ,, |
| U. Dorfeuillianus. | ,, | U. Medellinus. | ,, |
| U. uromas. | ,, | U. Menkianus. | ,, |
| U. ebenus. | ,, | U. metanever. | ,, |
| U. elegans. | ,, | U. Mühlfeldianus. | ,, |
| U. ellipsis. | ,, | U. multiplicatus. | ,, |
| U. multiradiatus. | ,, | U. subovatus. | ,, |
| U. modolioformis. | ,, | U. subrotundus. | ,, |
| U. notatus. | ,, | U. sulcatus. | ,, |
| U. Novi-Eboraci. | ,, | U. Taitianus. | ,, |

| U. obesus. | *Lea.* | U. Tampicoensis. | *Lea.* |
|---|---|---|---|
| U. obsurus. | ,, | U. Tappanianus. | ,, |
| U. occidens. | ,, | U. teniassimus. | ,, |
| U. palliatus. | ,, | U. trapezoides. | ,, |
| U. patulus. | ,, | U. trigonus. | ,, |
| U. stapes. | ,, | U. Troostensis. | ,, |
| U. perdix. | ,, | U. turgidus. | ,, |
| U. perplexus. | ,, | U. Vanuxemensis. | ,, |
| U. pictus. | ,, | U. varicosus. | ,, |
| U. pileus. | ,, | U. Vaughanianus. | ,, |
| U. pliciferus. | ,, | U. venustus. | ,, |
| U. pulcher. | ,, | U. Watercensis. | ,, |
| U. pumilis. | ,, | U. Zeiglerianus. | ,, |
| U. pustulatus. | ,, | U. zigzag. | ,, |
| U. pustulosus. | ,, | U. alatus. | *Say.* |
| U. pyramidatus. | ,, . | U. apiculatus. | ,, |
| U. Rangianus. | ,, | U. camptodon. | ,, |
| U. Ravenelianus. | ,, | U. cariosus. | ,, |
| U. Roanokensis. | ,, | U. crassus. | ,, |
| U. rubigunosus. | ,, | U. cylindricus. | ,, |
| U. Schoolcraftensis. | ,, | U. declivis. | ,, |
| U. securis. | ,, | U. dehiscens. | ,, |
| U. Shepardianus. | ,, | U. monodontus. | ,, |
| U. simus. | ,, | U. nasutus. | ,, |
| U. solidus. | ,, | U. ovatus. | ,, |
| U. Sowerbianus. | ,, | U. personatus. | ,, |
| U. spinosus. | ,, | U. subtentus. | ,, |
| U. splendidus. | ,, | U. tetralasmus. | ,, |

## 2. Genus *Hyria.*

*Animal.* As above.

*Shell.* Solid, nacred, equivalve, obliquely triangular, auriculated; base straight and truncated; hinge with two projecting teeth, the cardinal divided into numerous radiations, anterior ones smaller, the others lamellar and long. Inhabits the lakes and rivers of America. Two species.

Hyria avicularis.                    Hyria corrugata.

### 3. Genus *Anodonta.*

*Animal.* As above.

*Shell.* Rather thin, regular, close, equivalve, inequilateral; summit anterodorsal; hinge entirely without teeth, with a post-apicial lamina; ligament external, dorsal and postapicial, two well marked muscular impressions, besides those of the retractile muscles. Inhabits fresh-water lakes in Europe and America. Forty-nine living species; and many fossil.

| | |
|---|---|
| Anodonta areolatus. | Anodonta anatina. |
| A. marginata. | A. sinuosa. |
| A. rubens. | A. Patagonica. |
| A. anatina. | A. cygnæa. |
| A. fragilis. | A. sulcata. |
| A. trapezialis. | A. cataracta. |
| A. rubens. | A. exotica. |
| A. uniopsis. | A. crispata. |
| A. intermedia. | A. Pennsylvanica. |
| A. glauca. | A. maximus. |

The following species are American.

| | | | |
|---|---|---|---|
| Anodonta magnifica. | *Lea.* | Anodonta gigantea. | *Lea.* |
| A. Woodiana. | ,, | A. incerta. | ,, |
| A. angulata. | ,, | A. Pepiniana. | ,, |
| A. Benedictensis. | ,, | A. plana. | ,, |
| A. cylindracea. | ,, | A. salmonia. | ,, |
| A. decora. | ,, | A. Stewartiana. | ,, |
| A. edentula. | ,, | A. subcylindracea. | ,, |
| A. Ferussacina. | ,, | A. Wahlamatensis. | ,, |
| A. fluviatilis. | ,, | A. Wardiana. | ,, |
| A. Newtonensis. | ,, | A. gibbosa. | *Say.* |
| A. Nuttaliana. | ,, | A. grandis. | ,, |
| A. Oregonensis. | ,, | A. impura. | ,, |
| A. ovata. | ,, | A. suborbiculata. | ,, |
| A. pavonia. | ,, | A. undulata. | ,, |
| | | A. lugubris. | ,, |

#### 4. Genus *Iridina*.

*Animal.* As above.

*Shell.* Thin, oval, much elongated, inauriculated; hinge very long, linear, and crenulated throughout its length, ligament external and marginal; two distinct muscular impressions. Inhabits the Nile. Six species.

| | |
|---|---|
| Iridina exotica, | Iridina Nilotica, |
| I. cælistis.* | I. elongata.* |
| I. rubens,* | I. McMurtria.* |

### FAMILY XIV.

#### CHAMACEA. Three genera,

#### 1. Genus *Diceras.*

*Animal.*

*Shell.* Inequivalve, adherent; beaks conical, very large, diverging in irregular spiral contortions; hinge with a large, thick, concave, subauricular tooth in the larger prominent valve; two muscular impressions. One species. Fossil.

Diceras arietina.

#### 2. Genus *Chama.*

*Animal.* Body suborbicular terminated superiorly by a sort of hook; mantle very slightly opened for the passage of a foot, terminated at its extremity by a part much narrower than the base; superior lobes of the branchiæ very short.

*Shell.* Irregular, adhering, inequivalve, inequilateral; summits more or less twisted spirally, especially in the lower valve by which these animals have the faculty of affixing themselves to other bodies; hinge dissimilar, thick, formed by a single lamellous tooth arcuated, subcrenulated, postcardinal and articulated in a furrow of the same form; ligament exterior and postapical; two large muscular impressions, distant. Seventeen living species. Eight fossil species.

| | |
|---|---|
| Chama damæcornis. | Chama Florida.* |
| C. crenulata. | C. æruginosa. |
| C. arcinella. | C. decussata. |
| C. cristella. | C. ruderalis. |

| | |
|---|---|
| C. Lazarus. | C. Japonica. |
| C. gryphoides. | C. limbula. |
| C. unicornis. | C. asperella. |
| C. radians. | C. albida. |

C. croceata.

### 3. Genus *Etheria.*

*Animal.* Unknown.

*Shell.* Adhering, irregular, thick, much nacred, inequilateral, inequivalve; summits subcephalic, thick, indistinct, in a species of heel, growing longer with age; hinge without teeth, callous, irregular and thick; ligament subdorsal in the exterior portion of the shell, and prolonged to a point internally; two irregular oblong muscular impressions, one superior and subposterior, the other inferior and anterior, with a marginal palleal impression Inhabits the Indian Ocean. Five species.

| | |
|---|---|
| Etheria elliptica. | Etheria semilunata. |
| E. trigonula, | E. transversa. |

E. carteronii.

## FAMILY XV.

### TRIDACNEA. Two genera.

### 1. Genus *Tridacna.*

*Animal.* Body somewhat thick; edges inflated, lobes of the mantle adhering, and united in nearly all their circumference, so as to present but three apertures, the first inferior and anterior, for the egress of the foot, the second superior and posterior for the branchial cavity, the third much smaller and in the middle of the dorsal edge; two pairs of labial appendages, thin, nearly filiform, in the middle of which is a very small buccal orifice; branchiæ long and narrow; abdominal muscular mass considerable, and giving issue, as if from a cup, to a thick bundle of byssoid muscular fibres.

*Shell.* Thick, solid, of variable size, regular triangular, inequilateral; summits inclined posteriorly, hinge dissimilar, entirely anterior to the summit; a lamellous precardinal tooth and two distant lateral teeth upon the left valve, corresponding with two precardinal lamellous teeth, and one distant lateral tooth upon the right valve ; ligament anterior, elongated ; a large, bifid ; submedian muscular impression ; another anterior one smaller and less distinct. Inhabits the Indian ocean. Six living species. One fossil species.

|  |  |
|---|---|
| Tridacna gigas. | Tridacna crocea. |
| T. squamosa. | T. mutica. |
| T. elongata. | T. serrifera. |

### 2. Genus *Hippopus*.

*Animal.*   As above.

*Shell.*   More elongated and inequilateral than in the *Tridacna*, the anterior side being longer than the posterior ; the posterior slope closed with a dentated margin. Inhabits the Indian seas. One species.

Hippopus maculatus.


## FAMILY XVI.

### Mytilacea.   Three genera.

#### 1. Genus *Mytilus*.

*Animal.*   Body oval, somewhat inflated ; mantle open in its inferior half only, and terminated posteriorly by an oval cleft with fringed edges ; a linguiform, canaliculated, abdominal appendage, with a byssus at its base behind, and several pairs of retractile muscles ; mouth with simple lips ; two contractile muscles, of which the anterior is very small.

*Shell.*   Of a serrated tissue, elongated more or less oval, sometimes subtriangular, equivalve, summits anterior, more or less curved, sloping inferiorly in a slight degree ; hinge toothless, or with two very small rudiments ; ligament dorsal, linear, subinterior inserted in a narrow and very long furrow ; two muscular impressions, of which the anterior is very small, besides those of the retractile muscles. Inhabits the British seas. Thirty-six species.

Mytilus erosus.          Mytilus Magellicanus.

M. decussatus.          M. crenatus.
M. elongatus.           M. hirsutus.
M. Zonarius.            M. latus.
M. violaceus.           M. ungulatus.
M. smaragdinus.         M. opalus.
M. edulis.              M. corneus.
M. Hesperianus.         M. retusus.
M. exustus.             M. perna.
M. ovalis.              M. bilocularis.
M. Domingensis.         M. ustulatus.
M. Afer.                M. Senegalensis.
M. ungularis.           M. achatinus.
M. borealis.            M. planulatus.
M. angustanus.          M. Galloprovincialis.
M. lacunatus.           M. lineatus.
M. incurvatus.          M. canalis.
M. abbreviatus,         M. sanguineus,

### 2. Genus *Modiola.*

*Animal.* As above.

*Shell.* Smooth, subtransverse, equivalve, regular, subtriangular, posterior side short ; summits nearly lateral ; hinge toothless, linear and lateral ; ligament partly interior, situated in a marginal furrow ; one sublateral, elongated muscular impression in each valve. Inhabits the British seas. Twenty-five species.

Modiola Guyanensis.      Modiola Papuana.
M. pulex.                M. tulipa.
M. discors.              M. albicosta.
M. cinnamorea.           M. vagina.
M. plicata.              M. picta.
M. lithophaga.           M. sulcata.
M. Adriatica.            M. plicatula.
M. discrepans.           M. semifusca.
M. trapezina.            M. purpurata.
M. silicula.             M. carbata.
M. semen.                M. caudigera.
M. lævigata.             M. squamosa.

M. securis.

### 3. Genus *Pinna*.

*Animal.* Body oval, elongated moderately thick enveloped in a mantle closed above, open below, and especially to the rear where it forms sometimes a sort of tube furnished with tentacular cirrhi : a flabelliform abdominal appendage, and a very considerable byssus ; mouth provided with double lips, beside two pairs of labial appendages ; a single large retractile muscle apparent.

*Shell.* Subcornate, fibrous, brittle, regular, equivalve, longitudinal, triangular, pointed anteriorly, in which direction is the summit, which is straight, wide, and frequently truncated posteriorly ; hinge dorsal, longitudinal, linear, toothless ; ligament occupying nearly all the dorsal edge of the shell ; a single and very wide muscular impression posteriorly ; a trace of the anterior in the summit. Inhabits the Mediterranean sea. Fifteen species.

| | |
|---|---|
| Pinna rudis. | Pinna flabellum. |
| P. seminuda. | P. angustina. |
| P. nobilis. | 'P. squamosa. |
| P. marginata. | P. muricata. |
| P. pectinata. | P. saccata. |
| P. ingens. | P. dolabrata. |
| P. varicosa. | P. vexillum. |
| P. nigrina. | |

## FAMILY XVII.

#### MALLEACEA. Five genera.

### 1. Genus *Crenatula*.

*Animal.* Unknown.

*Shell.* Irregular, much flattened, subrhomboidal, subequivalve, gaping posteriorly ; summit anterior ; hinge longitudinal, dorsal, toothless ; ligament submultiple, or inflated from place to place, and inserted in a series of round cavities corresponding with the dorsal edge ; muscular impression unique and subcentral. Inhabits the Red sea. Seven species.

| | |
|---|---|
| Crenatula modiolaris. | Crenatula bicostalis. |

C. avicularis.        C. viridis.
C. nigrina.           C. mytiloides.
        C. phasianoptera.


## 2. Genus *Perna*.

*Animal.* Body much compressed, the mantle prolonged posteriorly in a sort of lobe, and fringed at its inferior edge only; a byssus; a single contractile muscle.

*Shell.* Irregular, much compressed, subequivalve, form somewhat variable, gaping at the anterior part of its inferior edge; summit very small: hinge straight, vertical, buccal, toothless; ligament multiple, and inserted in a series of longitudinal and parallel furrows; a subcentral muscular impression. Inhabits the Indian seas. Ten species living. Two fossil; one found in France and one in Virginia.

Perna ephippium.        Perna sulcata.
P, isognomon.           P. vulsella.
P. femoralis.           P. nuclea.
P. marsupion.           P. avicularis.
P. obliqua.             P. canina.


## 3. Genus *Malleus*.

*Animal.* Imperfectly known, but certainly byssiferous, with a single retractile muscle.

*Shell.* Subnacreous, irregular, subequivalve, inequilateral, generally much auriculated anteriorly, and prolonged posteriorly into the body, so as to present some resemblance to a hammer; summits entirely anterior; between them and the inferior auricle, an oblique slope for the passage of the bissus: hinge linear, very long, buccal, toothless; ligament simple, triangular, inserted in a conical oblique pit, partly external; a moderately large subcentral muscular impression. Inhabits the Australian seas. Six species.

Malleus normalis.        Malleus vulsellatus.
M. vulgaris.             M. anatinus.
M. albus.                M. decurtatus.

### 4. Genus *Avicula.*

*Animal.* Body much compressed; mantle cleft throughout its circumference, except along the back, and garnished at its free edge with a double row of very short tentacular cirrhi; foot small, canaliculated; a byssus; mouth surrounded with fringed lips, besides two pair of labial appendages, a large contractile muscle, nearly posterior.

*Shell.* Foliaceous or not; always nacred, subequivalve, of a subregular form, but somewhat variable; valves oblique, the left one with a little notch, through which the byssus passes; hinge linear, toothless, or with two small rudimentary teeth; ligament more or less exterior, placed in a narrow groove; one very large posterior muscular impression and one very small anterior. Inhabits the coast of Devonshire. Fourteen species.

| | |
|---|---|
| Avicula nudata. | Avicula lotaria. |
| A. macroptera. | A. heteroptera. |
| A. semi-sagitta. | A. crocea. |
| A. falcata. | A. Atlantica. |
| A. Tarentina. | A. papilionacea. |
| A. squamulosa. | A. physoides. |
| A. costellata. | A. virens. |

### 5. Genus *Meleagrina.*

*Animal.* As above.

*Shell.* Subequivalve, rounded, squamous, a sinus posteriorly for the passage of the byssus, at which place the left valve is notched and narrow; hinge linear and destitute of teeth; ligament marginal, elongated, partly exterior, and dilated in the centre. Inhabits the Indian ocean. Two species, of which our first is the pearl-oyster.

| | |
|---|---|
| Meleagrina margaritifera. | Meleagrina albina. |

## FAMILY XVIII.

### PECTINEA. Seven genera.

### 1. Genus *Pedum.*

*Animal.* Unknown, but probably byssiferous.

*Shell.* Subtriangular, inequilateral, inequivalve, with rounded summits, feebly marked, unequal and distant : the right valve inflated, widened at its inferior and posterior edge, sloped anteriorly, and subauriculated, the left not being so ; hinge toothless, anterior or buccal ; ligament inserted in an oblique cavity prolonged outwardly to the summits, and carried within into a spoonlike cavity. Inhabits the Indian ocean. One species.

Pedum spondyloideum.

## 2. Genus *Lima.*

*Animal.* Body moderately compressed ; a byssiferous abdominal appendage ; edges of the mantle furnished with tentacular cirrhi in several rows; mouth surrounded with a very thick fringed lip.

*Shell.* Oval, more or less oblique, nearly equivalve, subauriculated, regularly gaping at the anterior portion of the inferior edge ; summits anterior and distant ; hinge buccal, longitudinal, toothless ; ligament rounded, nearly exterior, inserted in an excavation in each valve ; a central muscular impression, divided into three very distinct parts. Inhabits the Indian, Australasian, American, and Mediterranean seas. Six living species. Eleven fossil.

| | |
|---|---|
| Lima inflata. | Lima glacialis. |
| L. squamosa. | L. fragilis. |
| L. annulata. | L. linguatula. |

## 2. Genus *Pecten.*

*Animal.* Body more or less compressed, orbicular ; mantle furnished with a single row of tentacular papillæ, and with small oculiform, pedunculated disks, with regular spaces between them ; rudiment of a canaliculated foot, and a byssus ; mouth surrounded with fleshy appendages, irregularly ramified.

*Shell.* Free, regular, thin, solid, equivalve, equilateral, auriculated ; summits contiguous ; hinge toothless, a ligamentous membrane throughout all its extent, besides a short, thick, ligament, almost altogether internal, and filling a triangular excavation under the summit; a single subcentral muscular impression.

8

Fifty-nine species—and, according to Defrance, ninety-eight fossil.

| | |
|---|---|
| Pecten maximus. | Pecten turgidus. |
| P. Jacobæus. | P. aspersus. |
| P. bifrons. | P. plicus. |
| P. zigzag. | P. rastellus. |
| P. medius. | P. flagellasus. |
| P. Latirentii. | P. flavidulus. |
| P. pleuronectes. | P. Japanicus. |
| P. purpuratus. | P. radulus. |
| P. pallius. | P. pes-felis. |
| P. imbricatus. | P. sauciatus. |
| P. asperimus. | P. aurantius. |
| P. varius. | P. sinuosus. |
| P. glaber. | P. virgo. |
| P. grisens. | P. Isabella. |
| P. flabellatus. | ' P. flexuosa. |
| P. quadradiatus. | P. inflexus. |
| P. Tranquebaricus. | P. miniaceus. |
| P. hybridus. | P. lividus. |
| P. obliteratus. | P. sulcatus. |
| P. Magellanicus. | P. unicolor. |
| P. lineolaris. | P. distans. |
| P. nodosus. | P. irradians. |
| P. pusio. | P. dispar. |
| P. gibbus. | P. Islandicus. |
| P. ornatus. | P. sulphureus. |
| P. florens. | P. pellucidus. |
| P. opercularis. | P. sanguineous. |
| P. tigris. | P. senatorius. |
| P. histrionicus. | P. lunatus. |

P. lineatus.

#### 4. Genus *Plagiostoma.*

*Animal.* Entirely unknown.

*Shell.* Moderately thick, regular, free, subequivalve, subauriculated, the two valves nearly equally dilated, both provided with a distinct summit reflexed to the middle of a plane surface.

with a large triangular slope in the middle; articulation transverse, straight, and by two distant lateral condylæ. Ten species. Fossils only.

### 5. Genus *Plicatula.*

*Animal.* Unknown.

*Shell.* Solid, adhering, subirregular, inauriculated, inequivalve pointed at the summit, rounded and subplicated posteriorly; inferior valve without heel; hinge cephalic, longitudinal, provided upon each valve with two strong teeth, entering in corresponding cavities; ligament altogether internal and inserted in a median cavity. Inhabits the American seas. Five species.

| | |
|---|---|
| Plicatula ramosa. | Plicatula cristata. |
| P. depressa. | P. Australis. |

P. reniformis.

### 6. Genus *Spondylus.*

*Animal.* Body moderately compressed, provided inferiorly with a rudiment of a foot, without byssus; mantle open in all its inferior and superior portion; mouth surrounded with very thick and fringed lips.

*Shell.* Solid, adhering, subregular, more or less spined, subauriculated, inequivalve; the right or inferior valve fixed, much more excavated than the other, and having posteriorly at the summit a triangular face enlarging, and elongating with age; hinge longitudinal, provided in each valve, with two strong teeth entering corresponding cavities; ligament short, nearly median, partly exterior; muscular impression single and subdorsal. Found in all the seas of hot climates, and even in the Mediterranean. Four of five fossils are found in France, one in South America. Twenty-one species.

| | |
|---|---|
| *Spondylus Americanus. | Spondylus gædaropus. |
| S. candidus. | S. arachnoides. |
| S. coccineus. | S. multilamellatus. |
| S. spathuliferus. | S. crassisquama. |
| S. longitudinalis. | S. ducalis. |
| S. costatus. | S. violascens. |

S. longispinous.        S. microlepos.
S. regius.              S. crocens.
S. variegatus.          S. radians.
S. avicularis.          S. aurantius.
S. zonalis.

### 7. Genus *Podopsis*.

*Animal.* Unknown.

*Shell.* Subregular, somewhat thick, equilateral, symmetrical, inequivalve, adhering by the extremity of the shorter valve; the other terminating in a pointed, reflexed, and median summit. Two fossil species.

## FAMILY XIX.

### OSTRACEA. Six genera.

### 1. Genus *Ostrea*.

*Animal.* Body compressed, more or less orbicular; edges of the mantle thick, not adhering or retractile, and provided with a double row of short and numerous tentacular filaments; two pairs of elongated and triangular labial appendages; a subcentral bipartite muscle.

*Shell.* Irregular, inequivalve, inequilateral, roughly foliaceous the left or inferior valve adhering, larger and deeper than the other, its summit prolonged with age into a sort of heel; the right or superior valve more or less operculiform; hinge oral, toothless; ligament subinterior, short, inserted in an oblong cardinal cavity increasing with the summit; muscular impression single and subcentral. Found in all seas near the mouths of rivers. Defrance enumerates one-hundred and twenty species. Lamarck thirty-three fossil, forty-eight living.

Ostrea edulis.          Ostrea ruscuriana.
O. borealis.            O. Canadensis.
O. cochlear.            O. mytiloides.
O. gallina.             O. trapezina.
O. lingua.              O. rufa.

O. Braziliana.

O. rostralis.

O. denticulata.

O. cornucopiæ.

O. doridella.

O. limacella.

O. hippopus.

O. Adriatica.

O. cristata.

O. numisma.

O. tulipa.

O. scabra.

O. parasitica.

O. spathulata.

O. cucullata.

O. rubella.

O. erucella.

O. labrella.

O. radiata.

O. gibbosa.

O. elliptica.

O. deformis.

O. plicatula.

O. fusca.

O. cristagalli.

O. virginica.

O. excavata.

O. sinuata.

O. tuberculata.

O. magaritacea.

O. Australis.

O. haliotidæa.

O. fucorum.

O. glaucina.

O. turbinata.

O. folia.

O. hyotis.

O. imbricata.

## 2. Genus *Gryphæa.*

*Animal.* Unknown.

*Shell.* More finely lamellated than in the *Ostrea*, free, or slightly adhering, subequilateral, very inequivalve; the inferior valve very concave, with a summit more or less recurved in a hook; the superior opiculiform and much smaller; hinge toothless; ligament inserted in an elongated and arcuated cavity; a single muscular impression. Habitation unknown. One species.

Gryphæa angulata.

## 3. Genus *Vulsella.*

*Animal.* Body elongated and compressed; mantle much prolonged posteriorly, and edged with two rows of very close tubercular papillæ; a moderately-large abdominal foot, proboscidiform, canaliculated, without byssus; a very large transversal mouth with well-developed triangular labial appendages; branchiæ narrow, very long, and united in nearly all their extent.

8*

*Shell.* Subnacred, irregular, flat, elongated, subequivalve, inequilateral, with summits anterior, distant and flexed inferiorly; hinge oral and toothless; ligament undivided, thick, inserted in a round pit excavated in a projecting apophysis upon each valve; a moderately large subcentral muscular impression, and two very small ones altogether anterior. Inhabits the Indian and Australasian seas. Six living species. One fossil.

| | |
|---|---|
| Vulsella hians. | Vulsella lingulata. |
| V. rugosa. | V. mytilina. |
| V. spongiarum. | V. ævata. |

### 4. Genus *Placuna*.

*Animal.* Entirely unknown.

*Shell.* Free, subirregular, very fine, almost entirely translucid, flat, subequivalve, subequilateral, slightly auriculated; hinge altogether internal, formed upon the superior valve, which is the smaller, by two elongated, unequal, oblique, crests; converging to the summit, at the internal side of which a ligament is attached in the form of a V., a single, small, subcentral muscular impression. Inhabits the Indian seas. Two fossils in France. Three living species.

| | |
|---|---|
| Placuna sella. | Placuna papyracea. |
| P. placenta. | |

### 5. Genus *Anomia*.

*Animal.* Much compressed; edges of the mantle very fine; not adhering, and furnished exteriorly with a row of tentacular filaments; contractile muscle thick, divided into three parts, the largest of which passes partially across a slope of the inferior valve, and often contains a calcareous substance or small bone, adhering to marine bodies.

*Shell.* Adhering, irregular, inequivalve, inequilateral, ostraceous; inferior valve a little flatter than the superior, divided at the summit into two sloping branches, whose approxmiation forms a large oval hole; the superior valve, which is the larger, has an oval excavation under the summit; a subcentral muscular impression, divided into three parts. Inhabits the British coasts. Nine species.

| | |
|---|---|
| Anomia ephippium. | Anomia cepa. |
| A. patellaris. | A. electrica. |
| A. pyriformis. | A. membranacea. |
| A. fornicata. | A. squamula. |

A. lens.

## FAMILY XX.

### Brachiopoda. Three genera.

#### 1. Genus *Orbicula.*

*Animal.* Body much compressed and rounded; mantle open throughout its whole circumference; two ciliated tentacular appendages.

*Shell.* Orbicular, much compressed, inequilateral, very inequivalve; inferior valve very thin, adhering, imperforated, the superior patelloid, with the summit more or less inclined towards the posterior side. Inhabits the Norwegian seas. One living species. Two fossil.

Orbicula Norwegica.

#### 2. Genus *Terebratula.*

*Animal.* Depressed, circular or oval, more or less elongated, with two long pectinated labial tentacula.

*Shell.* Thin, inequivalve, regular, subtrigonal; one of the valves larger and more dilated than the other, which is sometimes operculiform; hinge condyloid, in a straight line and formed by two oblique articular surfaces in one valve placed between corresponding projections in the other. Inhabits the sea at the Zetland Islands. Twelve living species. Thirty-seven fossil.

| | |
|---|---|
| Terebratula dilatata. | Terabratula globosa. |
| T. flavescens. | T. caput-serpentis. |
| T. dorsata. | T. psittacea. |
| T. Vitrea. | T. rotunda. |
| T. dentata. | T. pisa. |
| T. sanguinea. | T. truncata.* |

### 3. Genus *Lingula.*

*Animal.* Depressed, oval, somewhat elongated, inclosed between two lobes of a mantle, slit throughout its anterior half, and having pectinated branchiæ adhering to the internal surface ; mouth simple, having on each side a long tentacular appendage ciliated in all its external edge, and rolling itself up spirally in the shell.

*Shell.* With an epidermis, subequivalve, equilateral, depressed, elongated, truncated anteriorly ; the summit median and posterior ; no trace of ligament ; a long fibro-gelatinous peduncle fixing the shell vertically to submarine bodies ; muscular impression multiple. Inhabits the Indian Ocean. One species.

Lingula anatina.

---

# CLASS IV.

## M O L L U S C A.

Animals soft, inarticulated, furnished with an anterior head, projecting or salient; most frequently with eyes and tentaculæ, or possessing, at their summit, arms disposed in the form of a coronet: their mouth either short, elongated, or tubular, exertile, and generally armed with hard parts. Mantle diversified, having its edges free on the sides of the body, or the lobes united, forming a sack, which in part envelopes the animal ; gills or respiratory organs various, circulation double, one particular, the other general; heart unilocular, sometimes with the auricles divided, and very distant; no medullary cord along the body, but scattered nerves and ganglions. Twenty-two families.

## FAMILY I.

### PTEROPODA. Six genera.

Some genera of this family are without a testaceous covering, mentioned only to preserve the family entire.

## 1. Genus *Hyalæa.*

*Animal.* Body enclosed in a shell, winged before, two opposite wings, somewhat retractile, inserted at the sides of the mouth, head distinct, mouth terminal, placed at the junction of the fins without eyes.

*Shell.* Symmetrical, very thin and transparent, valves unequal, flat above, convex below, open like a cleft anteriorly, summit truncated and tridentated posteriorly. Inhabits the Mediterranean. Two species.

Hyalæa tridentata.          Hyalæa cuspidata.

## 2. Genus *Clio.*

*Animal.* Body free, naked, more or less elongated, tapering to the rear, head very distinct; provided with six long conical retractile tentaculæ, separated into two groups of three each ; mouth altogether terminal and vertical, eyes sessile, rudiment of a foot under the neck.

This is a molluscous animal without any testaceous covering, but is here placed as leading to other genera which have shells. Inhabits the Indian seas. Two species.

Clio borealis.          Clio Australis.

## 3. Genus *Cleodora.*

*Animal.* Body oblong, gelatinous, contractile ; a head in front with two wings, and the posterior part enveloped in a shell, head distinct, projecting and round ; two eyes ; mouth in the form of a small beak ; destitute of tentaculæ ; two opposite membranaceous pellucid, and cordated wings, placed at the base of the neck.

*Shell.* Pyramidal, triangular, of a gelatinous or cartilaginous substance, very thin and transparent ; aperture obliquely truncated. Inhabits the South American seas. Two species.

Cleodora pyramidata.          Cleodora caudata.

## 4. Genus *Limacina.*

*Animal.* Body soft, oblong, two branchial fins situated at the base of the neck ; posterior part of the body spiral, and enveloped in a shell.

*Shell.* Thin, fragile, papyraceous, spiral, the whorls reunited in a planorbis form, and deeply and largely umbilicated on one side, aperture large and entire. Inhabits the north seas. One species.

Limacina helicialis.

### 5. Genus *Cymbulia.*

*Animal.* Body oblong, gelatinous, pellucid, enclosing a shell; head sessile; two eyes, and two retractile tentacula; mouth with a retractile proboscis; two opposite oblong ovate, branched wings, connate at their posterior base.

*Shell.* Gelatinous, cartilaginous, very transparent, crystalline, oblong, in shape of a shoe, from which it has derived the name of the slipper, truncated at the summit; aperture lateral and anterior. Inhabits the Mediterranean. One species.

Cymbulia Peronii.

### 6. Genus *Pneumodermon.*

A Molluscous animal, whithout any testaceous covering, and much resembling the genus Clio. Inhabits the Indian seas. One species.

Pneumodermon Peronii.

## FAMILY II.

### PHYLLIDIACEA. Six genera.

### 1. Genus *Phyllidia.*

A mollusca similar to the preceding genus, without a shell, but its back covered with a rough or coriaceous skin. Inhabits the Mediterranean. Three species.

Phyllidea varicosa.　　　　Phyllidea pustulosa.
P. ocellata.

### 2. Genus *Chitonellus.*

*Animal.* Body creeping, elongated; middle of the back provided its entire length with a detached multivalve shell; the alternate pieces for the most part longitudinal ; sides naked ; branchiæ disposed around the body ; foot cleft longitudinally by a deep furrow.

*Shell.* Each valve with striæ radiating from its apex ; the margins serrated ; the base of the last valve obtuse. The testaceous plates of this genus are never joined like those of the chiton, so that the animal can move in every direction. Upon the contraction of the animal after death, however, these valves become nearly united. Inhabits the seas of New Holland. Two species.

Chitonellus striatus. Chitonellus larvæformis.

### 3. Genus *Chiton.*

*Animal.* Body creeping, ovate oblong, convex, round at both extremities ; marginated with a coriaceous skin ; the back covered by a longitudinal series of testaceous, transverse, imbricated, and moveable plates ; head before, sessile, with the mouth placed below, destitute of tentacula or eyes ; branchiæ placed round the body, under the margin of the skin ; and orifice at the posterior extremity.

*Shell.* Eight imbricated valves, nearly smooth, slightly carinated, and rounded at the margins: summit more or less marked and curved, by longitudinal elongations. Inhabits the British and American coasts. Sixty species.

| | |
|---|---|
| Chiton fulvus. | Chiton gigas. |
| C. pisceus. | C. squamosus. |
| C. ruber. | C. Peruvianus. |
| C. lævis. | C. tesselatus. |
| C. spinosus. | C. capensis. |
| C. fascicularis. | C. Carmichaelis. |
| C. marginatus. | C. echinatus. |
| C. crinitus. | C. striatus. |
| C. siculus. | C. lineolatus. |
| C. niger. | C. chilensis. |
| C. spiniferous. | C. tuberculatus. |
| C. coquimbensis. | C. hispidus. |
| C. lumingii. | C. thalassimus. |
| C. granosus. | C. porosus. |

C. glauco-sinctus.

C. disjunctus.

C. elegans.

C. lineatus.

C. sulcatus.

C. bicolor.

C. cerasimus.

C. Magellanicus.

C. marmoratus.

C. nebulosus.

C. olivaceous.

C. latus.

C. punctatus.

C. viridus.

C. cinerus.

C. tunicatus.

C. larvaformis.

C. undulatus.

C. luteolus.

C. fuscus.

C. minimus.

C. cimex.

C. ascellus.

C. Icelandicus.

C. fasciatus.

C. setosus.

C. variegatus.

C. asselloides.

C. indus.

C. albas.

C. castaneus.

*C. Emersonii.

*C. fulminatus.

## 4. Genus *Patella.*

*Animal.* Body completely covered by the shell; head with two acute tentaculæ, and the eyes situated at their exterior base; branchiæ placed under the mantle and around the body.  ·

*Shell.* This numerous and beautiful genus of Linnæus has been subdivided into the several distinct genera of Fissurella, Emarginula, Navicella, Umbrella, Pileopsis, Calyptrea, Crepidula, Parmophora, and Ancylus; each of which possesses sufficiently well-defined characters to authorize a separation, by which they may be more easily distinguished from the still widely extended family of Patella. Oval, conic, or a little depressed, outside green or brown, sometimes radiated with various colors; having divergent striæ and concentric wrinkles, inside glossy, iridescent, with yellow or fawn colored, purple, blue, or brown radiations. Inhabits the coast of Europe. Forty-five species.

Patella safiana.

P. testitudinaria.

P. cochlear.

P. compressa.

P. Australis.

P. apicina.

P. granatina.

P. oculus.

P. granularis.

P. decaurata.

P. Magellanica.

P. stellifera.

P. vulgata.

P. Mammillaris.

P. lineata.

P. leucopleura.

P. notata.

P. Tarentina.

P. punctata.

P. puncturata.

P. Javanica.

P. tuberculifera.

P. miniata.

P. pellucida.

P. tricostata.

P. Galathia.

P. pectinata.

P. viridula.

P. scutellaris.

P. radians.

P. cærulea.

P. plumbia.

P. umbrella.

P. pyramidata.

P. luteola.

P. aspera.

P. spinifera.

P. longicosta.

P. barbata.

P. angulosa.

P. saccharina.

P. laciniosa.

P. plicata.

### 5. Genus *Umbrella*. Pl. IX.

*Animal.* Body very thick and oval, provided with a dorsal shell; foot large, smooth and flat, surrounded by a border, anteriorly notched, attenuated behind; head indistinct; four tentacula, the two upper ones thick, short, and truncated, the other two thin, and shaped like pedunculated crests; having foliaceous branchiæ.

*Shell.* External, orbicular, subirregular, nearly flat, slightly convex above, white, with apex near the middle; margin acute, internal surface rather concave; having a callous disk, coloured, depressed in the centre, surrounded by a smooth border. Inhabits the Indian Ocean. Two species.

Umbrella Indica.          Umbrella Mediterranea.

### 6. Genus *Pleurobranchus*. Pl. IX.

*Animal.* Body creeping, fleshy; mantle and foot expanded; branchiæ placed on the right side; cloak enveloping the shell; neck short, contracted in some species, with an emarginate front,

9

exhibiting the commencement of the inferior tentacula, the upper ones, tubular and cloven; gills at the edge of the dorsal plait, mouth provided with a short retractile proboscis.

*Shell.* Depressed oval oblong, concentrically wrinkled, almost entirely open, rounded and convoluted; the vertex with a single turn. Inhabits the coast of Devonshire in England. Two species.

Pleurobranchus Peronii.     Pleurobranchus Laqueare.

## FAMILY III.

CALYPTRACEA.   Seven genera.

### 1. Genus *Parmophorus*.   Pl. IX.

*Animal.* Body creeping, thick, oblong ovate, broad behind, obtuse at the extremities; border of the mantle cleft before, and suspended vertically around; head distinct, and slit below; two conical contracted tentacula, at the base of which are placed the eyes, which are somewhat pedunculated; mouth below, funnel shaped, oblique, truncated and concealed; branchial cavity opening anteriorly behind the head by a transverse fissure.

*Shell.* Oblong, very depressed, slightly convex above, obtuse at extremities, anteriorly channeled by a slight sinus, and having towards the posterior part a small pointed apex, inclined backwards; the lower surface slightly concave. Inhabits the Australian seas. Four species.

Parmophorus Australis.     Parmophorus granulata.

P. brevicula.               P. ambigua.

One fossil species.

### 2. Genus *Emarginula*.   Pl. IX.

*Animal.* Body creeping, with two conical tentacular, eyes at the external vase; mantle large, partly covering the margin of the shell; foot very large and thick.

*Shell.* Shield-like, conical; summit inclined; the cavity simple, having a notch or hollow cut on its posterior margin; shells of

this genus are generally very small, Inhabits the British seas.
Five species.

Emarginula Blainvillii.         Emarginula fissura.

E. Cuvierii.                    E. rubra.

E. marginata.

### 3. Genus *Fissurella*. Pl. IX.

*Animal.* With the head truncated in front; two conical tentacula, with eyes at their exterior base; mouth simple, terminal,
and destitute of jaws; two pectinated branchiæ projecting from
the cavity; mantle large, protruding beyond the shell.

*Shell.* Shield shaped, conical recurved, summit entire, depressed, concave below, perforated at the summit in the form of a key
hole, without a spire, the exterior surface ribbed longitudinally.
Inhabits the European seas.   Twenty species.

Fissurella Cayenensis.          Fissurella Javanicensis.

F. lilacina.                    F. fascicularis.

F. rosea.                       F. pustula.

F. Barbadensis.                 F. hiantula.

F. radiata.                     F. viridula.

F. nodosa.                      F. depressa.

F. nimbosa.                     F. Peruviana.

F. crassa.                      F. gibberula.

F. Græca.                       F. minuta.

F. picta.                       F. plicata.

### 4. Genus *Pileopsis*. Pl. X.

*Animal.* With two conical tentacula, and the eyes at their
base; branchiæ formed in a row under the anterior margin of the
cavity, near the neck.

*Shell.* Obliquely conical, anteriorly recurved, apex bent,
almost spiral; aperture rounded, elliptical, the anterior margin
shortest, acute, slightly sinuated; the posterior largest and rounded.
One elongated and arched muscular impression, situated under the
posterior margin.   Inhabits the seas of Europe.   Five species.

Pileopsis intorta.              Pileopsis ungarica.

P. subrufa.                     P. mitula.

P. depressa.

## 5. Genus *Calyptrea*. Pl. X.

*Animal.* The same as preceding genus.

*Shell.* This genus derives its common name, "the Cup and Saucer Limpit," by having in the interior cavity a cup shaped appendage, which is sometimes vertical, and sometimes like a horse shoe, with a muscular impression of variable form, vertex ending in a small volution; smooth, margin entire, very glossy within and provided with a laminar plate. Inhabits the Chinese seas. Eight species.

| | |
|---|---|
| Calyptrea porcellana. | Calyptrea equestris. |
| C. fornicata. | C. tecum-sinense. |
| C. peziza. | C. scutellata. |
| C. angulata. | C. poculum. |

## 6. Genus *Crepidula*. Pl. X.

*Animal.* Head anteriorly forked, having two conical tentacula, with the eyes placed at their exterior base; mouth simple, destitute of jaws, and situated in the bifurcation of the head; branchiæ with tufts and projecting from the branchial cavity; the mantle never bordering the shell; foot minute, orifice lateral.

*Shell.* Ovate, or oblong, the back almost always convex, concave beneath; the spire very much inclined towards the margin; the aperture partly closed by a horizontal lamina. Inhabits the American seas. Seven species.

| | |
|---|---|
| Crepidula extinctorum. | Crepidula uguiformis. |
| C. aculeata. | C. dilata. |
| C. lævigata. | C. Peruviana. |
| C. gigas. | |

## 7. Genus *Ancylus*. Pl. X.

*Animal.* Body creeping, enveloped in the shell; two compressed subtruncated tentacular, with eyes situated at their internal base; foot short, elliptical; somewhat narrower than the body.

*Shell.* Thin, obliquely conical; aperture oval, with a pointed apex, which very much inclines backwards, margins simple. This is a fresh water shell, found in the lakes of Europe and rivers of America. Three species.

Ancylus lacustris. Ancylus fluviatilis.

A. spinarosæ.

## FAMILY IV.

BULLACEA. Three genera.

### 1. Genus *Acera*.

*Animal.* Body ovate, convex, transversely divided above into two parts; the foot with dilations in the form of wings below; head indistinct; branchiæ situated on the back, greatly behind, and covered by a mantle destitute of a shell. Inhabits the Mediterranean. One species.

Acera carnosa.

### 2. Genus *Bullæa.* Pl. X.

*Animal.* Body ovate, somewhat convex above, and divided into two parts transversely; lateral lobes of the foot very thick; head indistinct, and without tentacula; branchiæ placed on the back.

*Shell.* Concealed in the mantle, very thin, rolled and spiral on one side; without a columella and spire; aperture very large and wide, dilated at the uper part. Inhabits the British seas. Two species.

Bullæa aperta. Bullæa striata.

### 3. Genus *Bulla.* Pl. X.

*Animal.* Body oblong ovate, slight convexity; divided into two portions transverse above, mantle slightly fold posteriorly; visible tentacula; branchiæ dorsal, and covered, opening only on the right side.

*Shell.* Univalve, ovate globular, convolute, no columella, spire not projecting but visible, aperture the whole length of the shell, external margin sharp and smooth. Inhabits the British seas. Fourteen species.

Bulla physis. Bulla fragilis.
B. naucum. B. aplustre.

O*

| | |
|---|---|
| B. hydatis. | B. ampulla. |
| B. rugosa. | B. lignaria. |
| B. fasciata. | B. solida. |
| B. striata. | B. cornea. |
| *B. Wyatii. | B. lactea. |

## FAMILY V.

### APLYSIACEA.   Two genera.

#### 1. Genus *Dolabella*.   Pl. X.

*Animal.* Body creeping, oblong, narrowed in front; and posteriorly widened; area round, sloping and truncated obliquely; margins folded over the back; four tubular tentacula, disposed in pairs; bronchial operculum inclosing a shell, orifice dorsal, near the branchiæ.

*Shell.* Oblong, slightly arcuated, thick, callous, and somewhat spiral, on both sides, singular in formation, and its characteristic unlike most other shells. Inhabits the Isle of France. Two species.

Dolabella Rumphii.        Dolabella fragilis.

#### 2. Genus *Aplysia*.   Pl. X.

*Animal.* Body creeping, oblong, convex above; bordered on each side by a broad mantle, which covers the back when the animal is in repose; head and neck elevated, with four tentacula, the two upper ones ear shaped, eyes situated near the mouth; dorsal shield simicircular, subcartilaginous, adhering on one side, and covering the branchial cavity.

*Shell.* Nearly round, left margin somewhat reflected; outer lip acute; yellowish horn colored, with brown radiations, and two concentric bands. Inhabits the Indian seas. Thirty-seven species.

| | |
|---|---|
| Aplysia depilans. | Aplysia hassetlii. |
| A. teremida. | A. punctata. |
| A. gigas. | A. marmorata. |

| | |
|---|---|
| A. dolabrifera. | A. kerandrenii. |
| A. ascifera. | A. lessonii. |
| A. petalifera. | A. camelus. |
| A. unguifera. | A. alba. |
| A. limacina. | A. Napolitana. |
| A. Jeachii. | A. viridis. |
| A. saviguana. | A. longicornis. |
| A. fasciata. | A. ecaudata. |
| A. bresili. | A. virescens. |
| A. dactycomela. | A. poliana. |
| A. protea. | A. fusca. |
| A. sorex. | A. pleii. |
| A. tigrina. | A. citrini. |
| A. maculanta. | A. undata. |
| A. longicanda. | A. rosea. |

A. ferrusacii.

## FAMILY VI.

Limacina. Five genera.

### 1. Genus *Limax*. Pl. X.

*Animal.* Cuvier merely mentions that the animal is "furnished with a coriaceous, subrogose shield, with a flat longitudinal disk beneath, four tentacula retractile, eyes at the tips, orifice for respiration on the right side."

*Shell.* Ovate oblong, both margins reflected; very thin, diaphanous, slightly wrinkled, of a pale yellow color. Inhabits the gardens in Britain and France. Five species.

| | |
|---|---|
| Limax rufus. | Limax albus. |
| L. cinerus. | L. agrestis. |

L. punctata.

### 2. Genus *Vitrina*. Pl. X.

*Animal.* Body creeping, elongated, snail shaped, nearly straight; posteriorly separated from the foot, and spirally wound into a shell.

*Shell.* Small, very thin, depressed, terminated above by a very short spire, the last whorl very large; aperture large, rounded oval; the left margin arched, slightly involute. Inhabits dry places of Europe. Three species.

Vitrina parilis. Vitrina dentilis.

V. pellucida.

### 3. Genus *Testacella.* Pl. X.

*Animal.* Body creeping, elongated, snail shaped, having a shell placed on the posterior extremity; four tentacula, the two longest with their eyes at their tips, respiratory organs behind.

*Shell.* Very small, external, ear shaped, apex absolutely spiral, aperture very large and oval, left edge sharp and rolled inward behind. Inhabits the middle provinces of France. Two species.

Testacella aliotidea. Testacella Neritoidea.

### 4. Genus *Parmacella.* Pl. X.

*Animal.* Body creeping oblong; middle of the back moderately convex, and shield shaped; hind part in form of a tail, laterally compressed, acute above; shield ovate, fleshy, adhering at its posterior part, free before, enveloping a shell, with a notch in the centre of its right margin, four tentacula, two posterior largest; respiratory organs, under the notch of the shield, placed between the two tentacula of the right side.

*Shell.* Ovate, left margin broad and reflected; right margin reflected at top and acute beneath; very thin and pellucid, of a pale yellowish brown. Inhabits the gardens of Europe. Two species.

Parmacella Olivieri. Parmacella Cuvierii.

### 5. Genus *Onchidium.* Pl. X.

*Animal.* Body oblong, creeping, marginated on all sides: head projecting, the lower part with a prominent margin, two retractile, cylindrical, tentacula; two auriform appendages, nearly lateral; mouth beneath, destitute of maxillary processes; respiratory orifices distinct, under the extremity of the body.

Destitute of a shell. Inhabits the gardens of Europe. Two species.

Onchidium Typhæ Onchidium Peronii.

## FAMILY VII.

*Colimacea.* Eleven genera.

### 1. Genus *Helix.* Pl. X.

*Animal.* Of a slightly variable form, the mantle forming at its free edge a kind of ring or thick collar, especially in front, and faintly divided into two lips; foot oval, plane, smooth beneath, inflated and granular below, joined to the visceral club by a narrow peduncle; head sufficiently distinct; anterior tentacula very evident and inflated at top, the posterior very long; the mouth a vertical cleft provided with two labial lobes, a sort of marginal tooth, and with a small, oval, lingual club.

*Shell.* The name Helix was given to this genus from the spiral shape of the shell, which varies much in form, but generally globular, and ventricose, conoid but never turriculated; summit generally obtuse, aperture varying much in size, sometimes very large, sometimes small, always regulated by the turn of the spire; oval, semilunar, more wide than long, edges disunited, entering little into the interior; right lip or margin thickened or reflected. Inhabits the groves and woods of Europe. One hundred and sixty-eight species.

| | |
|---|---|
| Helix vesicalis. | Helix cepa. |
| H. gigantea. | H. heteroclites. |
| H. polyzonalis. | H. discolor. |
| H. monozonalis. | H. lactea. |
| H. pulla | H. zonaria. |
| H. lineolata. | H. guttata. |
| H. mutata. | H. Madagascarensis. |
| H. pomatia. | H. Javanica. |
| H. aspersa. | H. Peruviana. |
| H. vermiculata. | H. simplex. |
| H. Alonensis. | H. cidaris. |
| H. vesicolor. | H. citrina. |
| H. naticoides. | H. algira. |
| H. picta. | H. verticellus. |

H. galactites.
H. hemastoma.
H. melanotragus.
H. extensa.
H. lucana.
H. globulus.
H. melanostoma.
H. cœlatura.
H. microstoma.
H. maculsa.
H. Richardi.
H. Bonplandii.
H. planulata.
H. labrella.
H. unguina.
H. pellis-serpentis.
H. senegalensis.
H. unidentata.
H. fructicum.
H. neglecta.
H. crespitum.
H. ericetorum.
H. intersecta.
H. carthusianella.
H. diaphana.
H. concolor.
H. velutina.
H. obvuluta.
H. Cookiana.
H. pileus.
H. papilla.
H. punctifera.
H. plicatula.
H. planorbella.
H. scabra.
H. cariosa.
H. crenulata.

H. olivetorum.
H. planospira.
H. Barbadensis.
H. sinuata.
H. hippocastanum.
H. bidentalis.
H. argilacea.
H. vittata.
H. arbustorum.
H. candidissima.
H. memoralis.
H. hortensis.
H. sylvatica.
H. pisana.
H. splendida.
H. serpentina.
H. niciensis.
H. variabilis.
H. auriculata.
H. turgidula.
H. helicella.
H. zonula.
H. tridentata.
H. septemvalva.
H. monodan.
H. fraterna.
H. coniformis.
H. concamerata.
H. nigrescens.
H. Tripolitana.
H. Sayii.
H. globulosa.
H. Caffra.
H. conformis.
H. prunum.
H. Pouzolzii.
H. contusa.

H. planorbula.

H. macularia.

H. maaitima.

H. strigata.

H. muralis.

H. rugosa.

H. cornea.

H. liquifera.

H. incarnata.

H. cinctella.

H. cellaria.

H. Gaymardii.

H. nitidia.

H. plebuim.

H. personata.

H. hispidia.

H. rotundata.

H. apicina.

H. striata.

H. conspurcata.

H. conica.

H. conoidea.

H. pulchella.

H. formosa.

H. orbiculata.

H. squamosa.

H. tectiformis.

H. Madeirensis.

H. bicarinata.

H. vitrinoides.

H. unbeculata.

H. Mitchelliana.*

H. Vancouverensis*

H. deformis.

H. Nicæensis.

H. meridionalis.

H. melitensis.

H. circumornata.

H. gronosa.

H. Lima.

H. dentiens.

H. parilis.

H. imperator.

H. zodiaca.

H. concisa.

H. pellicuta.

H. strobilus.

H. alanda.

H. carina.

H. Bulverii.

H. pileolus.

H. vipartita.

H. sinistrorsa.

H. fibula.

H. supplicata.

H. Porto-santara.

H. punctulata.

H. exalbida.

H. Caroliniensis.*

H. Nuttaliana.*

H. Columbiana.*

H. Californensis.*

H. Townsendiana.*

H. Nichliniana.*

H. Oregonensis.*

H. magnifica.*

2. Genus *Carocolla.* Pl. X.

The *Animal* of this and the following genera of this family are precisely the same as in Helix.

*Shell.* Orbicular, more or less convex or connoidal above; the circumference or periphery angulated or keeled; aperture transverse, contiguous to the axis of the shell; the right margin or lip subangular, often toothed or plaited beneath. Inhabits dry situations in Europe and America. Twenty-two species.

Carocolla acutistima.

C. albilabris.

C. angistoma.

C. labyrinthus.

C. lucerna.

C. inflata.

C. hispidula.

C. Gaulteriana.

C. albella.

*C. Hydiana.

*C. helicoides (new species) Lea.

Carocolla bicolor.

C. mauritiana.

C. Madagascarensis.

C. marginata.

C. lychnuchus.

C. planata.

C. planaria.

C. lapicida.

C. elegans.

*C. grata.

*C. Spinosa (new species) Lea.

### 3. Genus *Achatina.* Pl. X.

*Animal.* See Helix.

*Shell.* Variable in form, but generally subturriculated, oval or oblong, aperture entire, the right lip sharp, never reflected, columella smooth, of which the anterior extremity is always open and truncated. Inhabits South America. Twenty-two species.

Achatina perdix.

A. immaculata.

A. acuta.

A. Mauritania.

A. ustulata.

A. virginea.

A. glans.

A. Marminii.

A. fusco-lineata.

A. columnaria.

A. acicula.

Achatina zebra.

A. purpurea.

A. bicarinata,

A. castanea.

A. vexillum.

A. Priamus.

A. Peruviana.

A. albo-lineata.

A. fulminea.

A. folliculus.

A. oleacea.

### 4. Genus *Anostoma.* Pl. X.

*Animal.* See Helix.

*Shell.* Somewhat extraordinary in its formation, orbicular, the spire convex and obtuse, aperture round, dentated grinning, turned upwards to the side of the spire, margin of the lip reflected. Lakes in America. Three species.

Anostoma dentata.*          Anostoma depressa.*

A. globosa.*

### 5. Genus *Helicina.* Pl. X.

*Animal.* See Helix.

*Shell.* Terrestrial, distinguished only from the Helix by its columella being transverse callous; much depressed and diminished in thickness at the lower part, subliglobular, imperforate; aperture entire, demioval, margin acute, forming an angle at the lower base of the right lip; operculum corneous. Inhabits groves in Europe. Nineteen species.

Helicina neritella.          Helicina rhodostoma.

H. striata.          H. major.

H. fasciata.          H. minima.

H. virida.          H. submarginata.

H. pulchella.          H. unifasciata.

H. substriata.          H. Brownii.

H. Braziliensis.          H. depressa.

H. costata.          H. aureola.

H. aurantia.          H. orbiculata.

H. Tankervillii.

### 6. Genus *Pupa.* Pl. X.

*Animal.* See Helix.

*Shell.* Cylindrical, generally thick; aperture irregular, semiovate, rounded, and subangulated beneath; margins of outer lip nearly equal and reflected outwardly, unconnected at their upper parts; the plait of the columella interposed between them. Inhabits moss generally in Europe. Thirty-three species.

Pupa numia.          Pupa quadridens.

P. uva.          P. polyodon.

P. sulcata.          P. variabilis.

P. candida.          P. frumentum.

10

P. labrossa.  P. secale.
P. fusus.  P. avena.
P. tridentata.  P. granum.
P. fasciolata.  P. fragilis.
P. zebra.  P. dolium.
P. unicarinata.  P umbilicata.
P. maculosa.  P. muscorum.
P. clavulata.  P. angilicus.
P. ovularis.  P. rufescens.
P. Garmanica.  P. edontulus.
P. cinerea.  P. odontostoma.
P. tridens.  P. petiveriana.

P. dentata.

### 7. Genus *Clausilia*. Pl. X.

*Animal.* See Helix.

*Shell.* Cylindrical, generally fusiform; summit obtuse, the last whorl smaller than the preceding; aperture irregular, rounded, oval; margin united, and externally reflected. Inhabits dry situations both in Europe and America. Fifteen species.

Clausilia torticollis.  Clausilia denticulata.
C. truncatula.  C. collaris.
C. retusa.  C. papillaris.
C. costulata.  C. plicatula.
C. corrugata.  C. rugosa.
C. inflata.  C. gracilis.
C. teres.*  C. chrysalis.

C. Mediterranea.

### 8. Genus *Bulimus*. Pl. X.

*Animals* of this genus, in formation are precisely as the Helix, they are, however, oviparous, producing eggs with the shell containing the animal perfectly matured; they are frequently as large as a pigeon's egg.

*Shell.* Oval, sometimes turriculated, oblong; the summit of the spire obtuse, and the last whorl larger than all the others together; aperture oblong, oval, edge disunited; in adults the lip much reflected; columella smooth, with an inflection in the middle, the base entire, not channelled. Inhabits mountainous situations in Europe; some beautiful specimens have been found in the woods of Ohio. Sixty one species.

Bulimus ovatus.
B. hæmastomus.
B. gallina.
B. sultana.
B. zigzag.
B. undatus.
B. Richii.
B. inversus.
B. citrinus.
B. sultanus.
B. Pythogaster.
B. ovoideus.
B. interruptus.
B. Peruvianus.
B. Favannii.
B. Kambeul.
B. papyraceus.
B. calcareus.
B. decollatus.
B. Lyonetianus.
B. inflatus.
B. radiatus.
B. fragilis.
B. Gaudalupinsis.
B. Mexicanus.
*B. glandiformis.
*B. parvus.
*B. virgo.
*B. gracilis.
*B. Gibbonius.

Bulimus multifasciatus.
B. Bengalensis.
B. Caribæorum.
B. octonus.
B. terebraster.
B. articulatus.
B. acutus.
B. scobinatus.
B. planidens.
B. ventricosus.
B. montanus.
B. hordaceus.
B. lubricus.
B. iostoma.
B. geniostoma.
B. odontostoma.
B. formosus.
B. Listeri.
B. Kingii.
B. Dufresnii.
B. pulcher.
B. maugeri.
B. lævis.
B. auris leporis.
B. vexillum.
*B. maculatus.
*B. lacteus.
*B. Pealianus.
*B. decoratus.
*B. Columbianus.

*B. corneus.

9. Genus *Succinea.* Pl. X.

*Animal.* See Helix.

*Shell.* Terrestrial, very thin, pellucid, ovate oblong, with a conical pointed spire, formed of only one or two whorls; aperture very large and oval, edges disunited; right edge always acute, the left arched, formed by a smooth attenuated columella. The shells of this genus never having their lip thickened or reflected, distinguish them from those of the genus Bulimus, to which they bear a strong resemblance. Inhabits the sides of ditches and lakes, both in Europe and America. Seven species.

| | |
|---|---|
| Succinea cuculata. | Succinea oblonga. |
| S. amphibia. | S. patula. |
| S. rubescens. | S. pellucida. |
| *S. aperta. | |

### 10. Genus *Auricula.* Pl. X.

*Animal.* See Helix.

*Shell.* Solid, thick, and smooth, oval, oblong spire very obtuse, aperture entire, enlarged, ear shaped, much contracted behind; edges not united, right lip thick and generally reflected outwardly; the left or columella with one or more teeth or callous plaits. This genus derives its name from its resemblance to the ears of certain animals. It is a land shell found chiefly in the East and West India Islands. Sixteen species.

| | |
|---|---|
| Auricula midæ. | Auricula scarabæus. |
| A. Judæ. | A. bovina. |
| A. sileni. | A. caprella. |
| A. leporis. | A. myosotis. |
| A. felis. | A. minima. |
| A. Dombeiana. | A. coniformis. |
| A. nitens. | A. monill. |
| A. angiostoma. | A. labrella. |

### 11. Genus *Cyclostoma.* Pl. X.

*Animal.* See Helix.

*Shell.* Terrestrial, distinguished from the preceding genera by a perfectly round aperture, reflected lip, and horny operculum, summit papillose; left edge having its origin very detached from the spire. Inhabits the East Indies. Thirty-five species.

| | |
|---|---|
| Cyclostoma planorbula. | Cyclostoma rugosa. |

C. volvulus.

C. carinata.

C. sulcata.

C. unicarinata.

C. tricarinata.

C. obsoleta.

C. patulum.

C. truncatum.

C. pulchrum.

C. Jamaicense.

C. lineolata.

C. elongatum.

C. mirabile.

C. orbella.

C. aurantium.

C. mirabile.

C. labeo.

C. interrupta.

C. ambiqua.

C. semilabris.

C. flavula.

C. fasciata.

C. mumia.

C. quarternata.

C. ferruginea.

C. decussata.

C. mammillaris.

C. maculatum.

C. ligata.

C. elegans.

C. tortum.

*C. maculata.

*C. Popayana.

## FAMILY VIII.

LYMNACEA. Three genera.

1. Genus *Lymnea.* Pl. X.

*Animal.* See Helix.

*Shell.* Aquatic, oval, sometimes turrited ; spire produced, thin, smooth, edges disunited, the left with a very oblique plait rising on the columella, forming an oval aperture, destitute of an operculum. Inhabits the ponds of America and Europe. Seventeen species.

Lymnea columnaris.

L. stagnelis.

L. palustris.

L. auricularia.

L. ovata.

L. peregra.

L. rubiginosus.*

L. solida.*

Lymnea minuta.

L. luteola.

L. acuminata.

L. intermedia.

L. leucostoma.

L. Emmoniensis.*

L. lessoni.*

L. apacina.*

L. Virginiana.*

10*

## 2. Genus *Physa.* Pl. X.

*Animal.* See Helix.

*Shell.* General sinistral, oval, oblong, or globular, very smooth, spire prominent, aperture oval, contracted posteriorly, right edge sharp, columella twisting obliquely, and enlarging to join itself to the anterior part of the margin, the whorls turning to the left hand gives this shell the appellation of heterostrophe. Inhabits the ditches of America and Europe. Six species.

| | |
|---|---|
| Physa fontinalis. | Physa hypnorum. |
| P. castanea.* | P. subopaca. |
| P. decisa.* | P. aurea.* |

## 3. Genus *Planorbis.* Pl. X.

*Animal.* See Helix.

*Shell.* Discoid, spire depressed, or involuted almost in the same vertical plane, causing the shell to be drepressed on each side, aperture oblong, luniform, axis remote, margin not reflected; no operculum. Inhabits the lakes of America and Europe. Fourteen species.

| | |
|---|---|
| Planorbis cornu-arietis. | Planorbis orientalis. |
| P. corneus. | P. carinatus. |
| P. spirorbis. | P. lutescens. |
| P. hispidus. | P. nitidus. |
| P. angulatus. | P. imbricatus. |
| P. deformis. | P. contortus. |
| P. vortex. | P. lens.* |

## FAMILY IX.

### MELANIANA. Three genera.

## 1. Genus *Melania.* Pl. X.

*Animal.* See Helix.

*Shell.* Turreted; aperture entire, spire slightly pointed, margin of the whorls often surmounted by spires, columella smooth and arched, closed by a thin horn-like operculum, this is a fluviatile shell, often covered by a thick epidermis. Inhabits the rivers of India. Many fine species are found in America. Twenty-nine species.

| | |
|---|---|
| Melania inquinata. | Melania helvetica. |
| M. asperata. | M. lineata. |
| M. spinolusa. | M. Byronensis. |
| M. gronifera. | M. sulcata. |
| M. aurita. | M. lævigata. |
| M. lineolata. | M. clavis. |
| M. trunculata. | M. decollata. |
| M. carinefera. | M. amarula. |
| M. truncata. | M. thiarella. |
| M. coarctata. | M. fasciolata. |
| M. punctata. | M. lævissima. |
| M. subulata. | M. corrugata. |
| *M. Troostiana. | *M. plicifera. |
| *M. Sayii. | *M. tuberculata (*Lea*). |
| *M. subularis (*Lea*). | *M. elongata. ,, |
| *M. acuta. ,, | *M. plicata. |
| | *M. inflata. |

## 2. Genus *Pirena.* Pl. X.

*Animal.* Much elongated, mantle prolonged into a canal at the left side, but without distinct tube; foot short, oval, with an anterior marginal furrow; head terminated by a depressed proboscidiform muzzle; tentacula very distant, thickly annulated, dilated in the inferior half of their length, and having the eyes at the summit of this dilation; mouth a terminal and vertical slit, without labial tooth, and with a very small tongue; a single long and narrow branchia.

*Shell.* Distinguished from the preceding genus by having a sinus at the base, and another at the summit; turreted; aperture longitudinal, right lip sharp, base of the columella inclined to the right. Inhabits the rivers of India and Africa. Five species.

| | |
|---|---|
| Pirena terebralis. | Pirena aurita. |
| P. cancellata. | P. spinosa. |
| | P. granulosa. |

## 3. Genus *Melanopsis.* Pl. X,

*Animal.* As preceding genus.

*Shell.* The Melanopsis is distinguished from the Melanaia, by the columella being callous in the upper part, and the base truncated as in the Achatina, and differs from the Pirena in having only a sinus or widened opening at the base of the shell; aperture covered by a horny operculum. Inhabits the rivers of the Archipellago. Three species.

Melanopsis costata.        Melanopsis lævigata.

M. prærosa.

## FAMILY X.

PERISTOMIANA. Three genera.

### 1. Genus *Valvata*. Pl. X.

*Animal.* See Helix.

*Shell.* Found only in fresh water; subdiscoid or conoid, umbilicated spiral whorls rounded; angular at the summit; aperture round, not modified by the penultimate whorl; the margins sharp and united; operculum orbicular and horny. Inhabits the rivers of Europe and America. Two species.

Valvata piscinalis.        *Valvata arcnifera. (*Lea.*)

### 2. Genus *Paludina*. Pl. X.

*Animal.* See Helix.

*Shell.* Generally found in fresh water, though some species have been found where it is salt; conoid covered with a greenish epidermis; the whorls rounded or convex, spiral cavity modified by the last whorl; aperture rounded, oval, oblong, angular at the summit; margins united, acute, never reflected outwards, operculum orbicular and horny. Inhabits the rivers of America and Europe. Nineteen species.

| | |
|---|---|
| Paludina vivipara. | Paludina achatina. |
| P. Bengalensis. | P. Australis. |
| P. viridis. | P. impura. |
| P. Francesii. | P. muriatica. |
| *P. sinistrosa. | *P. hyalina. |

*P. Nuttaliana.      *P. unicolor.
*P. virens.      *P. nuclea.
*P. pallida.      *P. decisa.
*P. subcarinata.      *P. fuscus.
*P. Nickliniana.

### 3. Genus *Ampullaria*. Pl. X.

*Animal.* Inflated, globular, spiral; foot oval, with a trans-verse furrow at its anterior edge; head wide; tentacula superior, very long, conical and pointed; eyes situated at their external base, and supported upon a very apparent peduncle; mouth vertical, situated between two lips disposed in form of a horse shoe and forming a kind of muzzle; no superior tooth; a bristly lingual band, but not prolonged into the abdominal cavity; a very large respiratory cavity, divided in two by an incomplete horizontal partition.

Animals of this genus are oviparous; producing an egg nearly as large as that of a pigeon, in which is found the young animal complete, and in a perfectly formed shell.

*Shell.* This genus appears to partake of the characteristics, both of the Paludina and the Natica, being fluviatile and frequently attaining a large size; spire very short, the last whorl much larger than all the others together; globular, very ventricose, umbilicus small, forming a compressed funnel shaped aperture, without interior callosity; aperture longer than broad with margins united; columellar lip thickened, projecting and reflected over the umbilicus; operculum horny. Inhabits the rivers of Europe. Thirteen species.

Ampullaria vivipara.      Ampullaria rugosa.
A. fasciata.      A. canaliculata.
A. effusa.      A. Guinica.
A. virens.      A. carinata.
A. avellana.      A. intorta.
A. fragilis.      A. conica.
*A. Pealiana.

## FAMILY XI.

NERITACEA. Four genera.

### 1. Genus *Neritina.* Pl. X.

*Animal.* Globular; foot circular, thick, without a furrow anteriorly, or a lobe for the operculum posteriorly, with a bipartite
columellar muscle; conical tentaculæ; eyes subpedunculate at
their external side; mouth without labial tooth, but with a denticulated tongue prolonged into the visceral cavity; a single large
pectiniform branchia.

*Shell.* This genus was formerly classed with the Nerita, which
in form it much resembles, but from the circumstance of the latter
inhabiting the sea, and Neritinæ fresh water; it now forms a
separate genus, thin, smooth, or finely striated, in all the species
known, the right side of the aperture does not possess any crenula-
tions or teeth; the operculum is provided with a lateral tooth on
one side. Some species are armed with spines; aperture semicircular; left margin smooth and sharp; spire imperfect, generally
dissolved by the animal. Inhabits the fresh water rivers of
Europe. Twenty-eight species.

| | |
|---|---|
| Neritacea puversa. | Neritacea semiconica. |
| N. pulligera. | N. strigilata. |
| N. dubia. | N. meleagris. |
| N. zebra. | N. virginea. |
| N. zigzag. | N. fluviatilis. |
| N. gagates. | N. viridis. |
| N. lugubris. | N. Bætica. |
| N. lineolata. | N. Oweniana. |
| N. fasciata. | N. careosa. |
| N. Domingensis. | N. caffra. |
| N. auriculata. | N. Smithii. |
| N. crepidularia. | N. spinosa. |
| N. brevispina. | N. Oweni. |
| N. corona. | N. pulchella. |

## 2. Genus *Nerita*. Pl. X.

*Animal.* See Neritina.

*Shell.* Marine, but never spined, solid, semiglobular, flattened beneath, not imbilicated; aperture large, entire, semilunar, the external margin much hollowed,; the columella sharp and often dentated, operculum horny, subspiral, with a projecting tooth. Inhabits the seas of S. America and W. Indies. Twenty species.

| | |
|---|---|
| Nerita exuvia. | Nerita lineata. |
| N. textilis. | N. scabricosta. |
| N. undata. | N. plicata. |
| N. peloronta. | N. tassellata. |
| N. chlorostoma. | N. signata. |
| N. artata. | N. ornata. |
| N. polita. | N. Australis. |
| N. albicella. | N. rudis. |
| N. chamæleon. | N. Ascensionis. |
| N. versicolor. | N. Malaccensis. |

## 3. Genus *Navicella*. Pl. X.

*Animal.* Oval, not spiral, foot elliptical, very large, with a thin subpapillary edge, advanced rather anteriorly, without marginal furrow, but attached on each side to the visceral mass in all its posterior portion so as to form a sort of cavity open transversely behind; head very broad and semilunate; tentacula conical, contractile and distant; eyes subpedunculated at the external root of the tentacula; mouth large and longitudinal.

*Shell.* Fluviatile, elliptical, or oblong, convex above, summit straight, depressed to the margin, concave beneath, no columella, the columellar edge replaced by a sharp partition, covering part of the aperture; a sinus of its left extremity; muscular impression horse-shoe shaped, open in front and interrupted behind; thin calcareous operculum, with a sublate, lateral tooth adhering to the posterior margin. Inhabits rivers in the Isle of France. Four species.

| | |
|---|---|
| Navicella elliptica. | Navicella lineata. |
| N. tesselatus. | N. porcelaniea. |

### 4. Genera *Natica.* Pl. XI.

*Animal.* Oval, subspiral; foot profoundly and transversely bilobed anteriorly, and having a horny or calcareous operculum; head provided with long setaceous tentacula, flat and auriculated at the base; eyes sessile at the external side of the root of the tentacula; mouth armed with a labial tooth.

*Shell.* Marine, distinguished from the Nerita by having no teeth, and having an umbilicus modified by a collosity; very smooth and glossy, no epidermis, spire evident, but low, columellar edge not toothed; right edge without teeth; operculum calcareous and smooth, semispiral, with concentrical ribs, fitting a groove on the columella. Inhabits the W. Indian Ocean and American seas. Thirty-six species.

| | |
|---|---|
| Natica ampullaria. | Natica unifasciata. |
| N. plumbea. | N. lineata. |
| N. conica. | N. fulminata. |
| N. aurantia. | N. maculoso. |
| N. melanostoma. | N. vittata. |
| N. mamilla. | N. castanea. |
| N. mamillaris. | N. arachynoidea. |
| N. albumen. | N. zebra. |
| N. glaucina. | N. Marochiensis. |
| N. caurena. | N. Javanica. |
| N. cruentata. | N. zonarie. |
| N. millepunctata. | N. cancellata. |
| N. vitellus. | N. patula. |
| N. helvacea. | N. duplicata. |
| N. collaria. | N. intricata. |
| N. monilifera. | N. glabrata. |
| N. labrella. | N. Chinensis. |
| N. rufa. | *N. consolidata. |

## FAMILY XII.

JANTHINEA. One genus.

### 1. Genus *Janthina.* Pl. XI.

*Animal.* Of oval form, spiral provided with a circular concave foot, accompanied with a vesicular subcartilaginous mass, and natatory appendages on each side; head very thick; tentacula scarcely at all contractile; eyes situated beneath the extremity of long peduncles placed at the external side of the tentacula, and appearing to form a part of them; mouth at the extremity of a very thick proboscidiform muzzle, between two vertical, subcartilaginous lips furnished with sharp spines.

*Shell.* Of a beautiful violet colour, found in numbers floating on the surface of the ocean, suspended by a vesicular appendage which gives a rich purple stain. Extremely thin and fragile, spire low, lateral, pointed, with subcarinated whorls; aperture large, subangular, modified by the last whorl of the spire, edges disunited, the left formed by the columella, which is straight, continuing beyond the base, right edge sharp, with a sinus in the middle. Inhabits the Atlantic Ocean. Three species.

Janthina naticoides.        Janthina communis.
J. exigua.

## FAMILY XIII.

MACROSTOMIANA. Four genera.

### 1. Genus *Sigaretus.* Pl. XI.

*Animal.* Body oval, flat beneath; edges of the mantle vertical, thin, extending beyond the body in all directions, sloped anteriorly; the mantle itself dilated superiorly.

*Shell.* More or less thick, internal, without colour, much depressed, with a short, low, lateral spire; left edge of the aperture trenchant; two lateral muscular impressions very distant. Inhabits the Indian Ocean. Four species.

Sigaretus convexus.        Sigaretus cancellatus.
S. Haliotoideus.           S. lævigatus.

### 2. Genus *Stomatella.* Pl. XI.

*Animal.* Unknown.

*Shell.* Distinguished from the Stomatia by being destitute of a tranverse rib, orbicular, oblong earshaped, imperforate; aper-

11

ture entire, large, sublongitudinal; right lip effuse, dilated, open. Inhabits the Indian Ocean. Five species.

Stomatella imbricata.          Stomatella sulcifera.

S. rubra.                       S. auricula.

S. planulata.

### 3. Genus *Stomatia.* Pl. XI.

*Animal.* Unknown.

*Shell.* Earshaped, imperforate, spire prominent; aperture entire, large, oblong; right margin aad columella equally raised; a transverse and tuberculated rib on the back. Inhabits the Indian Ocean. Two species.

Stomatia phymotis.          Stomatia obscurata.

### 4. Genus *Haliotis.* Pl. XI.

*Animal.* Body oval, much depressed, slightly spiral posteriorly, provided with a large foot doubly fringed at its circumference; head depressed; tentacula a little flattened; eyes at the summit of prismatic peduncles situated at the external side of the tentacula; mantle very thin deeply slit at the left side; the two lobes pointed and forming by their union a kind of canal to conduct water into the branchial cavity, and including two very long unequal branchial combs.

*Shell.* This beautiful genus derives its name from its resemblance to the human ear. The exterior, tuberculated, and generally loaded with marine substances, giving it an uncouth appearance, but its irridescent interior forms a magnificent contrast; it is pearly, with all the hues of the rainbow, recurving very depressed, oval, spire very small, sometimes eroded, almost posterior, aperture as large as the shell, with margins reflected inwards, the right sharp, left flat, and enlarged; disk pierced with holes, disposed in a line parallel to and near the left margin, the last commencing with a notch. These holes formed by the animal, as it increases the size of the shell, to admit the passage of a short syphon; they adhere to rocks, and are removed with much difficulty. Inhabits the sea at Molucca. Nineteen species.

| | |
|---|---|
| Haliotis tuberculata. | Haliotis dubia. |
| H. striata. | H. iris. |
| H. asinina. | H. tubifera. |
| H. glabia. | H. excavata. |
| H. lamellosa. | H. australis. |
| H. unilateralis. | H. Midæ. |
| H. rugosa. | H. rubra. |
| H. canaliculata. | H. tricostata. |
| H. tricostalis. | H. corrugata. |

H. Mariæ.

## FAMILY XIV.

PLICACEA. Two genera.

### 1. Genus *Tornatella*. Pl. XI.

*Animal* Body oval, subspiral; foot divided into two heels by a wide transverse furrow; head provided with two vertical cylindrical tentacula, having the eyes placed sessilely upon their interior side.

*Shell.* Convolute, oval, cylindrical, mostly striated transversely; no epidermis; spire very short, last whorl much larger than all the others together; one or two large plaits on the columella Inhabits the coast of Britain. Six species.

| | |
|---|---|
| Tornatella fasciata. | Tornatella nitidula. |
| T. solidula. | T. pedipes. |
| T. auricula. | T. flammea. |

### 2. Genus *Pyramidella*. Pl. XI.

*Animal.* As preceding genus.

*Shell.* Smooth and turreted, without epidermis, elongated conical or subturriculated; aperture entire demioval; the outer lip sharp and dentated within, columella produced, subperforate at the base, furnished with transverse plaits. Inhabits the American and W. Indian seas. Six species.

| | |
|---|---|
| Pyramidella terrebellum. | Pyramidella maculosa. |
| P. dolabrata. | P. plicata. |
| P. corrugata. | P. ventricosa. |

# FAMILY XV.

Scalarina. Three genera.

## 1. Genus *Scalaria.* Pl. XI.

*Animal.* Spiral; foot short, oval, and inserted beneath the neck; two tentacula terminated by a filament, and having the eyes at the extremity of the dilated portion; a proboscis.

*Shell.* Marine, aperture circular, spire more or less pressed and furnished with longitudinal ribs, formed by the preservation of the reflected margin of the aperture; edges united, thickened, and outwardly reflected; operculum horny and thin. Inhabits the American and Indian seas. Eleven living species, and three fossil.

| | |
|---|---|
| Scalaria coronata. | Scalaria varicosa. |
| S. communis. | S. raricota. |
| S. Australis. | S. lamellosa. |
| S. tenebralis. | S. pretiosa. |
| S. Martinii.* | S. Novanglia * |
| S. subulata.* | |

## 2. Genus *Vermetus.* Pl. XI.

*Animal.* As preceding genus.

*Shell.* Very similar to the Serpula, but the organization of the animal makes it a distinct genus; often found clustered together and attached to marine substances; conical, thin tubular, loosely spiral, aperture straight, circular, edges sharp and complete, several partitions not perforated towards the summit, operculum horny and complete. Inhabits the sandy shores of the W. Indies and Africa. Two species.

Vermetus lumbricalis.    Vermetus maximus.

## 3. Genus *Delphinula.* Pl. XI.

*Animal.* See Scalaria.

*Shell.* Thick, and pearly in the interior subdiscoid or conical; spiral whorls rough or angular, often detached, spiny, large umbilicus, sometimes triangular; the margins united, mostly fringed or

ventricose. Inhabits the Indian seas. Four living species.
Seven fossil.

| | |
|---|---|
| Delphinula laciniata. | Delphinula distorta. |
| D. turbinopsis. | D. rugosa. |

## FAMILY XVI.

TURBINACEA. Eight genera.

### 1. Genus *Solarium.* Pl. XI.

*Animal.* Unknown.

*Shell.* Orbicular, depressed, umbilicus large and conical, crenulated or dentated on the inner margin of the whorls; aperture not modified by the last whorl of the spire, which is entirely flat; no columella. Inhabits the Indian seas. Seven living species. Eight fossil.

| | |
|---|---|
| Solarium granulatum. | Solarium lævigatum. |
| S. perspectivum. | S. stramineum. |
| S. hybridum. | S. variegatum. |
| S. luteum. | |

### 2. Genus *Trochus.* Pl. XI.

*Animal.* Spiral, having the sides of the body often ornamented with digitated or lobed appendages, and provided with a short foot rounded at its two extremities; head provided with two tentacula more or less elongated, having the eyes upon a dilation of their external base; mouth without superior tooth, but furnished with a spiral lingual band.

*Shell.* Marine, found in almost all parts of the world, some smooth, others knotted, spined, tuberculated, or undulated; thick, generally pearly, spire sometimes depressed, at others elevated and pointed at the summit, sharp or carinated at its circumference, frequently umbilicated, not always; aperture transversely depressed, the margins not united at the upper part; columella arched and twisted, often projecting forward; operculum horny, thin, with numerous spiral whorls, increasing from the centre to the circum-

11*

ference.    Inhabits the European seas.    Ninety-nine living specie Eight fossil.

| | |
|---|---|
| Trochus imperialis. | Trochus jujubinus. |
| T. longispina. | T. Javanicus. |
| T. solaris. | T. annulatus. |
| T. Indicus. | T. doliarius. |
| T. radians. | M. granulatus. |
| T. pileus. | T. granatum. |
| T. calyptræformis. | T. moniliferous. |
| T. fimbriatus. | T. iris. |
| T. brevispina. | T. ornatus. |
| T. rotularius. | T. bicingulatus. |
| T. stella. | T. calliferus. |
| T. stellarius. | T. umbilicaris. |
| T. asperatus. | T. undatus. |
| T. rhodostomus. | T. Pharaonis. |
| T. spinulosus. | T. sagittiferus. |
| T. costulatus. | T. carneolus. |
| T. inermis. | T. cinerarius. |
| T. agglutinans. | T. excavatus. |
| T. coelatus. | T. nanus. |
| T. tuber. | T. pyramidatus. |
| T. magus. | T. erythroleucos. |
| T. merula. | T. undosus. |
| T. argrostomus. | T. unguis. |
| T. cookii. | T. olivaceus. |
| T. niloticus. | T. Smithii. |
| T. pyramidalis. | T. maugeri. |
| T. noduliferas. | T. Mediterraneus. |
| T. cærulescens. | T. reticulatus. |
| T. obeliscus. | T. indistinctus. |
| T. virgatus. | T. pellioserpentis. |
| T. maculatus. | T. armillatus. |
| T. granosus. | T. acuminatus. |
| T. squarrosus. | T. elegantus. |
| T. incrassatus. | T. granosus. |
| T. flammulatis. | T. tæniatus. |

T. elatus.

T. marmorus.

T. mauritianus.

T. imbricatus.

T. triseliatus.

T. crenulatus.

T. asperulus.

T. acutus.

T. concavus.

T. lineatus.

T. zizyphinus.

T. conuloides.

T. conulus.

T. zonatus.

T. articulatus.

T. pictus.

T. callosus.

T. clanguloides.

T. interruptus.

T. lævis.

T. albidus.

T. celandii.

T. quadricostatus.

T. Byronianus.

T. elongatus.

T. filosus.

T. clangulus.

T. sulcatus.

T. Montagui.

### 3. Genus *Monodonta*. Pl. XI.

*Animal.* See Trochus.

*Shell.* This genus appears to be the connecting link between the Trochus and Turbo; distinguished from the former, by an entirely rounded aperture, slightly depressed; from the latter, by the toothlike projecting angle the truncated columella occasions at the base; an operculum. Inhabits the Chinese seas. Thirty-four species.

Monodonta bicolor.

M. pagodus.

M. tectum-persicum.

M. papillosa.

M. coronaria.

M. Ægyptiacea.

M. carchedonius.

M. modulus.

M. Listeri.

M. tectum.

M. labio.

M. australis.

M. canalifera.

Monodonta badia.

M. articulata.

M. lugubris.

M. punctulata.

M. caniculata.

M. seminigra.

M. rosea.

M. lineata.

M. rugosa.

M. zebra.

M. reticularis.

M. trochlea.

M. atrata.

M. viridis.

M. fragarioides.

M. constricta.

M. tricarinata.

M. obscura.

M. concamerata.

M. odontis.

M. pulcherrima.

### 4. Genus *Turbo*. Pl. XI.

*Animal.* Very similar to that of Trochus, the sides sometimes ornamented with tentacular appendages, varying in number and form; head proboscidiform; tentacula thin and setaceous.

*Shell.* Depressed conical, or subturreted; sometimes umbilicated, frequently carinated at its circumference; interior pearly; aperture round or depressed, the middle of external edge hollowed; edges rarely joined by a callosity; columella arched, rarely twisted, not truncated at the base; an operculum. Inhabits the Indian seas. Forty-three species.

Turbo marmoratus.

T. imperialis.

T. torquatus.

T. Sarmaticus.

T. cornutus.

T. argyrostomus.

T. chrysostomus.

T. radiatus.

T. setosus.

T. splenglerianus.

T. petholatus.

T. undulatus.

T. pica.

T. versicolor.

T. samaragdus.

T. cidaris.

T. diaphanus.

T. rugosus.

T. coronatus.

T. crenulatus.

T. margaritaceus.

Turbo muricatus.

T. littoreus.

T. ustulatus.

T. Nicobaricus.

T. neritoides.

T. retusus.

T. bicarinatus.

T. rudis.

T. obtusus.

T. pullus.

T. cærulescens.

T. cancellatus.

T. costatus.

T. niger.

T. minimus.

T. tuberculatus.

T. zebra.

T. pintado.

T. crassus.

T. fluctuatus.

T. hippocastanum.

T. saxosus.

### 5. Genus *Planaxis.* Pl. XI.

*Animal.* Unknown.

*Shell.* Ovate conical, solid; aperture ovate, sublongitudinal, columella flat and truncated at the base, separated from the right margin by a narrow sinus. Interior surface of the right margin furrowed or lineated, and a callosity running under the summit. Inhabits the American and W. Indian seas. Four species.

| | |
|---|---|
| Planaxis sulcata. | Planaxis bicolor. |
| P. undulata. | ⁎P. lævigatum. |

### 6. Genus *Phasianella.* Pl. XI.

*Animal.* Spiral; foot oval; upon each side an appendage ornamented with filaments; head edged anteriorly with a kind of veil formed by a double, bifid, fringed lip; two long conical tentacula; eyes borne upon short peduncles and situated at the external part of their base; mouth between two vertical subcornate lips.

*Shell.* Marine; many of them very rare and valuable; their beauty of colouring disposed so as to resemble the plumage of a pheasant. Oval, rather thick, smooth and glossy, spine pointed; columella uniting itself with the left edge, forming interiorly a londitudinal callosity; aperture oval, larger before, with edges disunited; operculum calcareous, oval, oblong, subspiral, the summit at one extremity. Inhabits the British coast. Twelve species.

| | |
|---|---|
| Phasianella varigata. | Phasianella sulcata. |
| P. rubens. | P. angulifera. |
| P. bulimoides. | P. lineolatus. |
| P. elegans. | P. perdix. |
| P. lineata. | P. Mauritania. |
| P. nebulosa. | P. Peruviana. |

### 7. Genus *Turritella.* Pl. XI.

*Animal.* Spiral; foot fringed anteriorly by a transversely wrinkled band; tentacular long, very fine towards their extremity somewhat thick at their base, and having the eyes upon an inflation; the head skirted with a veil or fringe garnished with filaments.

*Shell.* Turreted, not nacred, rather thin, striated in the direc tion of the decurrence of the spire; very pointed, and with numerous whorls; aperture rounded; the edges posteriorly, the right exceedingly thin, and slightly sinous towards the middle; operculum horny. Inhabits the Indian and American Oceans. Fourteen living species. Thirty-seven fossil.

| | |
|---|---|
| Turritella duplicata. | Turritella terebra. |
| · T. imbricata. | T. replicata. |
| T. fuscata. | T. cornea. |
| T. brevialis. | T. bicingulata. |
| T. trisulcata. | T. exoleta. |
| T. catinifera. | T. Australis. |
| T. Virginiana.* | T. saturalis.* |

### 8. Genus *Rotella*. Pl. XI.

*Animal.* See Turbo.

*Shell.* Orbicular, glossy, destitute of epidermis, spire short, subconic; lower parts convex and callous; aperture half round. Indian Ocean. Seven species.

| | |
|---|---|
| Rotella lineolata. | Rotella formosa. |
| R. Javanica. | R. saturalis. |
| R. rosea. | R. equalis. |

R. monolifera.

### FAMILY XVII.

CANALIFERA. Eleven genera.

### 1. Genus *Cerithium*. Pl. XI.

*Animal.* Much elongated; the mantle prolonged into a canal at its left side, but without a distinct tube; the foot short, oval, with an anterior marginal furrow; the head terminated by a depressed proboscidiform muzzle.

*Shell.* More or less turriculated and tuberculous; aperture small, oval, and oblique; the columellar edge much excavated and callous, the right edge trenchant, and slightly dilating with age. Operculum horny, oval, round, subspiral, and striated upon the external face. Inhabits the seas of N. Holland. Forty-one living species. Sixty fossil.

| | |
|---|---|
| Cerithium palustre. | C. fasciatum. |
| C. telescopium. | C. muricatum. |

C. nodulosum.

C. obeliscum.

C. aluco.

C. giganteum.

C. sulcatum.

C. ebeninum.

C. vulgatum.

C. granulatum.

C. echinatum.

C. subulatum.

C. zonale.

C. tortulosum.

C. morus.

C. erythæonense.

C. radula.

C. decollatum.

C. semigranosum.

C. lineatum.

C. cressum.

C. obtusum.

C. asperum.

C. vertagum.

C. literatum.

C. heteroclites.

C. semiferrugineum.

C. tuberculatum.

C. ocellatum.

C. atratum.

C. eburneum.

C. lima.

C. zonatum.

C. rugosum.

C. mitriforme.

C. punctatum.

C. perversum.

C. petrosum.

C. exasperatum.

## 2. Genus *Pleurotoma.* Pl. XI.

*Animal.* Body oval, spiral above, enveloped in a mantle of which the right edge is furnished with lobes ; foot oval and somewhat short ; eyes situated at the external base of long conical, retractile tentacula ; mouth having a long extensible proboscis armed with hooked teeth ; organs of respiration formed by two unequal branchiæ.

*Shell.* Fusiform, a little wrinkled, with a turriculated spire : a small oval aperture, terminated by a straight canal more or less long, with the right edge trenchant ; a horny operculum. Distinguished from the Cerithium by having a notch in the margin. Twenty-nine living species. Thirty fossil.

Pleurotoma muricata.

P. echinata.

P. flavidula.

P. imperialis.

P. auriculifera.

P. spirata.

Pleurotoma interrupta.

P. cincta.

P. crenularis.

P. unizonalis.

P. lineata.

P. fascialis.

| P. besirarginata. | P. buccinoides. |
| P. cingulifera. | P. virgo. |
| P. Babylonia. | P. undosa. |
| P. marmorata. | P. tigrina. |
| P. crispa. | F. albina. |
| P. nodifera. | P. mitra. |
| P. bicarinata. | P. elegans. |
| P. pleurotoma. | P. curvirostris. |

P. bicarinata.*

### 3. Genus *Turbinella*. Pl. XI.

*Animal.* Imperfectly known.

*Shell.* Usually turbinated (but sometimes turriculated), wrinkled, thick; spire slightly variable in form; aperture elongated, terminated by a straight canal, and often rather short; the left edge nearly straight and formed by a callosity concealing the columella, which has two or three nearly transverse and unequal folds; the right edge entire and trenchant. Found in the equatorial or Australian seas. Twenty-three species.

| Turbinella scolymus. | Turbinella ocellata. |
| T. napus. | T. rustica. |
| T. pugillaris. | T. polygonia. |
| T. rapa. | T. carinifera, |
| T. pyrum. | T. rhinoceros. |
| T. leucozonalis. | T. cornigera. |
| T. cingulifera. | T. ceramica. |
| T. mitis. | T. capitella. |
| T. infundibula. | T. globulus. |
| T. lineata. | T. craticulata. |
| T. triserialis. | T. nassatula. |

T. variolaris.

### 4. Genus *Cancellaria*. Pl. XI.

*Animal.* See *Purpura* hereafter.

*Shell.* Oval or globular, wrinkled; spire middling and pointed; aperture wide ovate, grooved, and sometimes canaliculated anteriorly; the right edge concave and trenchant; the left nearly straight and marked in the middle with two or three folds; operculum horny. Inhabits the Indian Ocean. Forty-eight living species. Twenty fossil.

Cancellaria crispa.
C. costifera.
C. articularis.
C. brevis.
C. pusilla.
C. bullata.
C. tuberculosa.
C. pulchra.
C. cancellata.
C. similis.
C. chrysostoma.
C. rugosa.
C. hæmastoma.
C. rigida.
C. costata.
C. goniostoma.
C. trigonostoma.
C. levigata.
C. spirata.
C. obliquata.
C. scalata.
C. contabulata.
C. crenifera.
C. scalarina.

Cancellaria littoriniformis.
C. elegans.
C. asperella.
C. oblonga.
C. tesselata.
C. nodulifera.
C. cassidiformis.
C. australis.
C. reticulata.
C. candida.
C. ovata.
C. Obesa.
C. acuminata.
C. solida.
C. gemmulata.
C. decussata.
C. indentata.
C. buccinoides.
C. clavatula.
C. uniplicata.
C. mitriformis.
C. tritonis.
C. granosa.
C. piscatoria.

### 5. Genus *Fasciolaria*. Pl. XI.

*Animal.* Entirely unknown.

*Shell.* Separated from the Murex on account of having no varix; fusiform or subfusiform; spire middling; aperture oval, elongated, nearly symmetrical, terminated by a rather long straight tube, the external edge trenchant, the columellar edge having two or three oblique folds. Inhabits the Indian Ocean and Mediterranean Sea. Eight living species. Seven fossil.

Fasciolaria trapezium.　　Fasciolaria ferruginea.

F. aurantiaca.          F. tarentina.

F. filamentosa.         F. tulipa.

F. coronata.            F. distans.

### 6. Genus *Fusus.* Pl. XI.

*Animal.*  Entirely unknown.

*Shell.*  With an epidermis, wrinkled, fusiform or dilated in the middle, prolonged posteriorly by the spire, and still more so anteriorly by the canal; aperture oval; the columellar edge straight or nearly so, the exterior trenchant; a horny and oval operculum. Inhabits the Indian and Northern seas.  Forty-two living species. Thirty-seven fossil.

Fusus aculeiformis.          Fusus Nicobaricus.

F. contrarius.               F. tortulosus.

F. longissimus.              F. multicarinatus.

F. laticosta.                F. antiquirus.

F. collosseus.               F. carinatus.

F. tuberculatus.             F. Islandicus.

F. distans.                  F. coronatus.

F. incrassatus.              F. corona.

F. sulcatus.                 F. filosus.

F. despectus.                F. verruculatus.

F. proboscidiferus.          F. Syracusanus.

F. morio.                    F. varius.

F. cochlidium.               F. afer.

F. raphanus.                 F. rubens.

F. polygonoides.             F. nifat.

F. lignarius.                F. buccinatus.

F. strigosus.                F. scalarinus.

F. crebricostatus.           F. sinistralis.

F. curvirostris.             F. articulatus.

F. inconstans.               F. pleurotomarius.*

F. colus.                    F. harpularis.*

### 7. Genus *Pyrula.* Pl. XI.

*Animal.*  Unknown.

*Shell.*  Pyriform on account of the depression of the spire, which distinguishes it from the Fusus; the canal conical, very long or middling, sometimes a little sloped; aperture oval, rather large; the columella edge somewhat excavated, entire and trenchant; an operculum. Found in the Northern seas. Twenty-nine living species. Six fossil.

| | |
|---|---|
| Pyrula salmo. | Pyrula plicata. |
| P. carica. | P. canaliculata. |
| P. candelabrum. | P. perversa. |
| P. tuba. | P. bucephala. |
| P. melongena. | P. vespertilio. |
| P. ficus. | P. reticulata. |
| P. spirata. | P. ficoides. |
| P. elongata. | P. spirillus. |
| P. bezoar. | P. ternatana. |
| P. papyracea. | P. rapa. |
| P. angulata. | P. galeodes. |
| P. nodosa. | P. squamosa. |
| P. abbreviata. | P. citrina. |
| P. deformis. | P. neritoidea. |

P. lineata.

### 8. Genus *Struthiolaria.* Pl. XI.

*Animal.* See Triton, hereafter.

*Shell.* Ovate; spire prolonged; aperture sinuous, terminated at the base by a very short straight canal; columellar edge callous; right edge having a thickened varix. Inhabits the Mediterranean and Northern seas. Two species.

Struthiolaria nodulosa. Struthiolaria crenulata.

### 9. Genus *Ranella.* Pl. XI.

*Animal.* Unknown.

*Shell.* Oval, and, as it were, depressed by the preservation of each side of a longitudinal thickened band; aperture oval, almost symmetrical by the excavation of the columellar edge, terminating anteriorly by a short canal, often a little sloping; a sinus at the posterior junction of the two edges. This genus forms a distinct division between the Murex and Struthiolaria. Inhabits the

Northern and Mediterranean seas. Fourteen living species. Five fossil.

| | |
|---|---|
| Ranella gigantea. | Ranella leucostoma. |
| R. candisata. | R. Argus. |
| R. ranina. | R. spinosa. |
| R. bufonia. | R. granulata. |
| R, granifera. | R. semigranosa. |
| R. bitubercularis. | R. crumena. |
| R. anceps. | R. pygmæa. |

### 10. Genus *Murex*. Pl. XI.

*Animal.* See *Pleurotoma*, above.

*Shell.* Usually oval; the spire but slightly elevated, roughened with longitudinal, transversal bands or varices; aperture small, quite oval, and symmetrical by the excavation of the left edge, formed by a lamina applied upon the columella, terminated anteriorly by a middling canal sometimes very long and closed; the right edge more or less furnished with varices. Operculum horny, complete, oval, nearly circular, with sub-concentric partitions; summit terminal. This genus comprehends only such shells as have only three or more varices on each whorl. These varices show how often the animal has increased the size of its shell. Found in all seas. Seventy-three living species. Two fossil.

| | |
|---|---|
| Murex cornutus. | Murex costularis. |
| M. tenuispina. | M. angularis. |
| M. ternispina. | M. cingulatus. |
| M. motacilla. | M. torosus. |
| M. palmarosæ. | M. granarius. |
| M. adustus. | M. aciculatus. |
| M. crevicornis. | M. ferrugo. |
| M. microphyllus. | M. pinnatus. |
| M. phylopterus. | M. triqueter. |
| M. trigonularis. | M. saxatilis. |
| M. brandaris. | M. melanomathos. |
| M. rarispina. | M. secundus. |
| M. haustellum. | M. trunculus. |
| M. inflatus. | M. Magellanicus. |

M. brevifrons.

M. rufus.

M. acaleatus.

M. capucinus.

M. acanthopterus.

M. ucinarius.

M. crassispina.

M. brevispina.

M. tenuirostrum.

M. elongatus.

M. calcitrassa.

M. axicornis.

M. longispina.

M. asperrimus.

M. tripterus.

M. hemitripterus.

M. gibbosus.

M. brassica.

M. radix.

M. scorpico.

M. turbinatus.

M. melonulus.

M. erinaceus.

M. tarentinus.

M. polygonulus.

M. crispatus.

M. cinguliferus.

M. lyratus.

M. fimbriatus.

M. regius.

M. funiculus.

M. pictus.

M. trigonulus.

M. endivia.

M. hexagonus.

M. quadrifrons.

M. anguliferus.

M. lamellosus.

M. scaber.

M. vitulinus.

M. fenestratus.

M. subcarinatus.

M. concatenatus.

M. pulchellus.

M. cristata.

M. lubiosus.

## 11. Genus *Triton*.  Pl. XI.

*Animal.* As above.

*Shell.* Oval with straight spire and canal, middling generally wrinkled, furnished with varices rare, scattered, and preserved in longitudinal rows; aperture suboval elongated, terminated by a short open canal; the columellar edge less excavated than the right and covered by a callosity; operculum horny, oval round and rather large. Found in the Northern and Mediterranean seas. Thirty-one living species. Three fossil.

Triton variegatum.

T. lampas.

T. corrugatum.

T. lotorium.

Triton tripus.

T. clavator.

T. chlorostomum.

T. subdistortum.

12*

T. cynocephalum.
T. retusum.
T. vespaceum.
T. clathratum.
T. maculosum.
T. cutaceum.
T. undosum.
T. nodiferum.
T. scorbiculator.
T. succinctum.
T. femorale.

T. clandestinum.
T. dolarium.
T. australe.
T. splengleri.
T. pileare.
T. pygrum.
T. canaliferum.
T. tuberosum.
T. annus.
T. cancellatum.
T. rubecula.

T. tranquebaricum.

## FAMILY XVIII.

### Alata.   Three genera.

#### 1. Genus *Rostellaria.*   Pl. XI.

*Animal.*   Entirely unknown.

*Shell.*   Subdepressed, turriculated, with a produced and pointed spire ; aperture oval on account of a rather large excavation of the columellar edge, the right margin dilating with age, and having a sinus contiguous to the pointed canal which terminates the shell ; an operculum.   This genus is distinguished from the Strombus by having a sinus in the lower part of the right margin contiguous to the canal.   Inhabits the European seas. Four living species.   Three fossil.

Rostellaria curvirostris.
R. rectirostris.

Rostellaria pespelicani.
R. cancellata.

#### 2. Genus *Pteroceras.*   Pl. XII.

*Animal.*   See Strombus, below.

*Shell.*   Oblong-ovate ; canal elongated, attenuated and often closed ; right margin dilating by age into an expanded digitated wing, attached to and covering a short spire with a sinus in the lower part not contiguous to the body.   Distinguished from the Strombus by not having the canal at the base shortened or truncated, and from the Rostellaria, by having the sinus of the right margin distant from the body. Found in the Equatorial seas. Seven species. Five fossil.

| | |
|---|---|
| Pteroceras truncata. | Pteroceras chiragra. |
| P. lambio. | P. millepeda. |
| P. scorpio. | P. pseudoscorpia. |
| P. aurantia. | |

### 3. Genus *Strombus*. Pl. XII.

*Animal.* Spiral; the foot rather wide anteriorly, compressed posteriorly; mantle thin, forming a prolonged fold anteriorly, whence issues a sort of canal; head very distinct; mouth a vertical slit at the extremity of a proboscis, provided in the inferior median line with a lingual band having prickles flexed posteriorly; tentacular appendages cylindrical thick and long, with the eyes at their extremity.

*Shell.* Thick, subinvolute, dilated in the middle, terminating in a cone anteriorly and posteriorly; aperture very long and narrow; terminated anteriorly by a canal more or less elongated and flexed; edges parallel, the external dilating with age, presenting posteriorly a gutter at its point of attachment with the spire, and, anteriorly, a sinus behind the canal, through which the head of the animal passes; operculum horny, long, and narrow; summit terminal. Found in the Indian and Equatorial seas. Thirty-two living species. Five fossil.

| | |
|---|---|
| Strombus gigas. | Strombus accipitrinus. |
| S. latissimus. | S. tricornis. |
| S. Canarium. | S. Isabella. |
| S. vittatus. | S. epidromis. |
| S. gallus. | S. bituberculatus. |
| S. cristatus. | S. dilatatus. |
| S. bubonius. | S. lentiginosus. |
| S. auris-Dianæ. | S. pugilis. |
| S. pyrulatus. | S. gibberulus. |
| S. Luhnanus. | S. Mauritianus. |
| S. colomba. | S. succinctus. |
| S. troglodytes. | S. tridentatus. |
| S. urceus. | S. plicatus. |
| S. Floridus.* | S. papilio. |

S. lineatus.                    S. marginatus.
S. turritus.                    S. cancellatus.

## FAMILY XIX.

PURPURIFERA.  Eleven genera.

### 1. Genus *Cassidaria*.  Pl. XII.

*Animal.*  Somewhat elongated, widened anteriorly; mantle
with simple edges and provided with a distinct tube; foot very
wide, elliptical, sub-bilolate anteriorly, and having a large operculum upon the dorsal face of its posterior part; head wide and indistinct; tentacula anterior, approximating at base, sub-cylin-
drical, and having the eyes at two-thirds of their length; mouth
inferior, concealed by the foot; two pectiniform branchiæ, nearly
parallel.

*Shell.*  Sub-globular, tuberculated or channelled, with a short
pointed spire; aperture long, ovate, subcanaliculated anteriorly;
right edge folded back; columella covered by a wide smooth
callosity uniting posteriorly with the right edge.  Inhabits all
seas except the Northern.  Five living species.  Seven fossil.

Cassidaria echinophora.         Cassidaria striata.
C. Tyrrhena.                    C. oniscus.
C. cingulata.

### 2. Genus *Cassis*.  Pl. XII.

*Animal.*  Spiral, with the foot (which is shorter than the shell)
rounded anteriorly; mantle provided, before the respiratory cavity,
with a long open canal, used as an organ of prehension; head
furnished; a single pair of blackish tentacula, having the eyes at
an inflation about half way from the base; mouth armed with a
proboscis.

*Shell.*  Inflated, oval, subinvolute; spire slightly projecting;
aperture long, oval, sometimes very narrow, terminated anteriorly
by a very short canal, sloped, and flexed obliquely towards the
back; columella covered by a large callosity, indented throughout
its length; operculum horny.  Found in the Indian, Mediterranean, and Equatorial seas.  Twenty-five living species.  Eight
fossil.

Cassis cornuta.

C. flammea.

C. rufa.

C. achatina.

C. areola.

C. abbreviata.

C. saburon.

C. Ceylonica.

C. erinaceus.

C. tuberosa.

C. fascinata.

C. pennata.

Cassis crumena.

C. zebra.

C. sulcosa.

C. canaliculata.

C. semigranosa.

C. Madagascariensis.

C. glauca.

C. testiculus.

C. plicaria.

C. decussata.

C. granulosa.

C. pyrum.

C. vibex.

### 3. Genus *Ricinula*. Pl. XII.

*Animal.* As above.

*Shell.* Oval or subglobular, thick, armed with points and with a depressed spire ; aperture narrow, elongated, notched, sometimes canaliculated anteriorly and digitated exteriorly ; left edge more or less callous; operculum horny, oval, and transverse. Found in the Indian seas. Nine living species.

Ricinula horrida.

R. arachnoidea.

R. digitata.

R. aspera.

Ricinula clathrata.

R. miticula.

R. pisolina.

R. morus.

R. mutica.

### 4. Genus *Purpura*. Pl. XII.

*Animal.* As above.

*Shell.* Oval, tuberculated, thick ; spire short, the last whorl much larger than all the others united ; aperture oval, greatly dilated, terminated anteriorly by a short, oblique canal notched at the extremity ; the columellar edge nearly straight, covered with a callosity ; operculum horny, flat, nearly semicircular, with faintly marked transverse striæ. Found in the European and South American seas. Fifty-five species.

Purpura Persica.

P. columellaria.

Purpura Francolinus.

P. cruentata.

P. armigera.

P. undata.

P. bufo.

P. planospira.

P. carinifera.

P. squamosa.

P. sertum.

P. ligata.

P. imbricata.

P. bicostalis.

P. thiarella.

P. echinulata.

P. unifascialis.

P. clavus.

P. bizonalis.

P. bulbus.

P. cariosa.

P. Rudolphi.

P. succincta.

P. bitubercularis.

P. hæmastoma.

P. callosa.

P. callifera.

P. scalariformis.

P. rugosa.

P. lagenaria.

P. plicata.

P. rustica.

P. hystrix.

P. retusa.

P. fasciolaris.

P. nucleus.

P. subrostrata.

P. patula.

P. consul.

P. hippocastana.

P. mancinella.

P. neritoides.

P. coronata.

P. sacella.

P. textilosa.

P. lambosa.

P. lapillus.

P. cateracta.

P. fiscella.

P. semi-imbricata.

P. deltoides.

P. trochlea.

P. vexillum.

P. distorta.

P. tectum.

### 5. Genus *Monoceros*.  Pl. XII.

*Animal.*   As above.

*Shell.* Differs only from the *Purpura* by a long, conical pointed, somewhat reflexed tooth in the outer lip.   Five species.

Monoceros cinqulatum.          Monoceros striatum.

M. imbricatum.                      M. glabratum.

M. crassilabrum.

### 6. Genus *Concholepas*.  Pl. XII.

*Animal.*   Entirely unknown.

*Shell.* Wide, rough, ovate; spire very short; aperture very large, oval and sloped anteriorly; the edges united, the right very thick and dentated; muscular impression almost in form of a horse-shoe : operculum horny and rudimentary. It was formerly, considered a Patella, from which it differs by the operculum. One species.

Concholepas Peruvianus.

7. Genus Harpa. Pl. XII.

*Animal* Unknown.

*Shell.* Oval, inflated, rather thin, with longitudinal parallel ribs formed by the preservation of the band of the right margin ; the spire very short and pointed, the last whorl much longer than all the others together; aperture large, ovate, with a wide slope anteriorly ; the right edge much hollowed, and thickened outwardly ; the columella smooth and terminated in a point anteriorly. A beautiful genus. Found in the Indian Ocean. Eight species.

| | |
|---|---|
| Harpa imperialis. | Harpa nobilis. |
| H. ventricosa. | H. articularis. |
| H. conoidalis. | H. rosea. |
| H. minor. | H. striata. |

8. Genus Dolium. Pl. XII.

*Animal.* As in *Purpura.*

*Shell.* Subglobular, thin, surrounded by decurrent flutings ; spire very short, the last whorl much larger than all the others together; aperture oblong, very large, on account of the great excavation of the right edge, which is crenated throughout its length ; columella twisted. Found in the Indian Ocean and Mediterranean seas. Seven species.

| | |
|---|---|
| Dolium galea. | Dolium variegatum. |
| D. fasciatum. | D. perdix. |
| D. pomum. | D. olearium. |
| | D. maculatum. |

9. Genus Buccinum. Pl. XII.

*Animal.* See Purpura.

*Shell.* With a light epidermis, oval, elongated; the spire moderately elevated; aperture oblong, oval, notched, sometimes subcanaliculated anteriorly; right edge thick, not reflexed; columella simple and dilated superiorly; operculum horny, complete and oval. Found in all seas. Fifty-eight living. Fourteen fossil.

| | |
|---|---|
| Buccinum undatum. | Buccinum tenniplicatum. |
| B. papyraceum. | B. levigatum. |
| B. crenulatum. | B. corniculatum. |
| B. lineatum. | B. Anglicanum. |
| B. maculosum. | B. lævissimum. |
| B. mutabile. | B. Tranquebaricum. |
| B. ventricosum. | B. lineolatum. |
| B. fasciatum. | B. suturale. |
| B. arcularia. | B. retusum. |
| B. pauperatum. | B. Caromandelianum. |
| B. achatinum. | B. lyratum. |
| B. olivaceum. | B. Thersites. |
| B. Brazilianum. | B. testudineum. |
| B. vinosum. | B. papillosum. |
| B. Ascanias. | B. tricarinatum. |
| B. aciculatum. | B. fasciolatum. |
| B. glaciale. | B. subspinosum. |
| B. annulatum. | B. flexuosum. |
| B. reticulatum. | B. cribarium. |
| B. fuscatum. | B. grana. |
| B. politum. | B. zebra. |
| B. inflatum. | B. aurantium. |
| B. gemmulatum. | B. gibbolusum. |
| B. miga. | B. marginulatum. |
| B. coronatum. | B. coccinella. |
| B. neriteum. | B. dermestoideum. |
| B. glans. | B. pediculare. |
| B. canaliculatum. | B. pullus. |
| B. semiconvexum. | B. polygonatum. |

10. Genus *Eburna.* Pl. XII.

*Animal.* Entirely unknown.

*Shell.* Oval or elongated, smooth; spire pointed, its whorls as if softened off; aperture ovate, elongated, widely notched anteriorly; the right margin entire; columella callous posteriorly, umbilicated, and subcanaliculated at its left side; an operculum. Found in the Indian and South American seas. Five species.

| | |
|---|---|
| Eburna glabrata. | Eburna spriata. |
| E. Ceylonica. | E. areolata. |
| E. lutosa. | |

## 11. Genus *Terebra.* Pl. XII.

*Animal.* Spiral and high; foot oval with a transverse anterior furrow, and two lateral auricles; head bordered with a small fringe; tentacula cylindrical, terminating in a point and very distant; eyes indistinct, situated at the root, and at the external side of the tentacula; mouth without proboscis; tube of the respiratory cavity very long.

*Shell.* Without epidermis, ovate, with a pointed spire, low, or subturriculated; aperture wide, oval, with a strong slope anteriorly; lower end of the columella twisted. Found in tropical seas. Twenty-four species.

| | |
|---|---|
| Terebra maculata. | Terebra Senegalensis. |
| T. crenulata. | T. cingulifera. |
| T. dimidiata. | T. scabrella. |
| T. raphanula. | T. lanceata. |
| T. muscaria. | T. granulosa. |
| T. flammea. | T. duplicata. |
| T. striatula. | T. corrugata. |
| T. chlorata. | T. cærulescens. |
| T. cerithina. | T. myuros. |
| T. subulata. | T. strigilata. |
| T. oculata. | T. aciculina. |
| T. Babylonica. | T. vittata. |

## FAMILY XX.

COLUMELLARIA. Five genera.

### 1. Genus *Columbella*. Pl. XII.

*Animal.* Imperfectly known; eyes placed much below the middle of the tentacula.

*Shell.* Thick, turbinated, with a short obtuse spire; aperture narrow, elongated and terminated by a very short canal, narrowed by an inflation at the inner side of the right edge, and by some folds on the columella; a very small horny operculum. Inhabits the Indian ocean. Eighteen species.

| | |
|---|---|
| Columbella rustica. | Columbella pardalina. |
| C. Hebræa. | C. ovulata. |
| C. semipunctata. | C. zonalis. |
| C. reticulata. | C. mendicaria. |
| C. strombiformis. | C. punctata. |
| C. mercatoria. | C. scripta. |
| C. flavida. | C. nitida. |
| C. bizonalis. | C. fulgurans. |
| C. turturina. | C. unifascialis. |

### 2. Genus *Mitra*. Pl. XII.

*Animal.* Entirely unknown.

*Shell.* Turriculated, subfusiform and oval; spire always pointed at the summit; aperture small, triangular, widest anteriorly where it is strongly emarginated; external edge trenchant, nearly straight, always longer than the columella, which is formed by a very thin callosity, and marked with oblique parallel folds, the anterior of which are the shortest; no operculum. Inhabits the Chinese seas. Eighty species.

| | |
|---|---|
| Mitra papalis. | Mitra crocata. |
| M. puncticulata. | M. nexilis. |
| M. cardinalis. | M. scabrinscrula. |
| M. versicolor. | M. crenifera. |

M. pedicula.
M. cornicularis.
M. striatula.
M. cornea.
M. melaniana.
M. episcopalis.
M. pontificalis.
M. millepora.
M. archiepiscopalis.
M. sanguinolenta.
M. lactea.
M. lutescens.
M. subulata.
M. tringa.
M. ferruginea.
M. adusta.
M. plicaria.
M. costellaris.
M. melongena.
M. vulpecula.
M. sanguisuga.
M. filosa.
M. amphorella.
M. patriarchalis.
M. harpæformus.
M. ficulina.
M. conularis.
M. dermestina.
M. dactylus.
M. conulus.
M. coronata.
M. muriculata.
M. semifasciata.
M. nucleola.
M. plumbea.
M. granulifera.

M. tæniata.
M. corrugata.
M. lyrata.
M. cinctella.
M. Caffra.
M. stigmataria.
M. fissurata.
M. clavula.
M. Peronii.
M. oniscina.
M. terebralis.
M. granulosa.
M. costa.
M. olivaria.
M. granatina.
M. serpentina.
M. arenosa.
M. literata.
M. obliquata.
M. scutulata.
M. fenestrata.
M. texturata.
M. limbifera.
M. paupercula.
M. torulosa.
M. retusa.
M. unifascialis.
M. larva.
M. tabanula.
M. crenulata.
M. aurantiaca.
M. cucumerina.
M. ebena.
M. microzonias.
M. bacilla.
M. pisolina.

### 3. Genus *Voluta.*　Pl. XII.

*Animal.*　Oval, involuted, provided with a very broad foot; head very distinct; tentacula rather short and triangular; eyes large, altogether sessile and situated a little posteriorly; a thick trunk furnished with hooked teeth at its extremity; two pectiniform branchiæ.

*Shell.*　Oval more or less ventricose; the first whorls of the spire rounded into a teat; aperture generally much longer than wide and sloping anteriorly; the right edge bent outwardly, entire and soft; the columellar edge garnished with large folds more or less oblique, and slightly varying in number with age. Found chiefly in the seas of the Torrid Zone.　Forty-four species.

| | |
|---|---|
| Voluta nautica. | Voluta Æthiopica. |
| V. armata. | V. imperialis |
| V. tesselata. | V. vespertilio. |
| V. cymbia. | V. musica. |
| V. proboscidalis. | V. levigata. |
| V. diadema. | V. nodulosa. |
| V. ducalis. | V. ancilla. |
| V. Neptuni. | V. Pacifica. |
| V. olla. | V. Junonia. |
| V. porcina. | V. melo. |
| V. pellis-serpentis. | V. Hebræa. |
| V. chlorosina. | V. serpentina. |
| V. polyzonalis. | V. carneolata. |
| V. magnifica. | V. fulva. |
| V. Magellanica. | V. nuclea. |
| V. fulminata. | V. lapponica. |
| V. scapha. | V. volvacea. |
| V. mitis. | V. mitræformis. |
| V. Braziliana. | V. nivosa. |
| V. Guinaica. | V. thiarella. |
| V. undulata. | V. sulcata. |
| V. festiva. | V. vexilla. |

### 4. Genus *Marginella.*　Pl. XII.

*Animal.*　Oval, involuted; foot elliptical, very large, and widest in front, where its edge presents a transverse furrow; head small, distinct, with two long, very sharp tentacula, the eyes at the external part of their base; mouth provided with a trunk.

*Shell.* Smooth, polished, oval-oblong, a little conical, with a short mammelonated spire; aperture somewhat narrow, slightly oval on account of a light curve of the right edge which is dilated outwardly; the columellar edge marked with three oblique distinct folds. Inhabits the Indian Ocean. Twenty-four living species and nine fossil, according to Defrance.

| | |
|---|---|
| Marginella radiata. | Marginella nubeculata. |
| M. limbata. | M. aurantia. |
| M. lifasciata. | M. longivaricosa. |
| M. dentifera. | M. eburnea. |
| M. bullata. | M. persicula. |
| M. avellana. | M. tessellata. |
| M. glabrella. | M. cærulescens. |
| M. quinqueplicata. | M. bivaricosa. |
| M. rosea. | M. muscaria. |
| M. faba. | M. formicula. |
| M. dactylus. | M. lineata. |
| M. cornea. | M. interrupta. |

### 5. Genus *Volvaria.* Pl. XII.

*Animal.* As above.

*Shell.* Cylindrical, convolute; spire obsolete or concealed; aperture narrow, extending the whole length of the shell, with one or more folds on the lower portion of the columella. Inhabits the Indian Ocean. Five species.

| | |
|---|---|
| Volvaria pallida. | Volvaria triticea. |
| V. monilis. | V. oryza. |
| | V. miliacea. |

## FAMILY XXI.

### CONVOLUTA. Six genera.

### 1. Genus *Cypræa.* Pl. XII.

*Animal.* Oval, elongated, involute; head provided with two

13*

very long conical tentacula; eyes at the extremity of an inflation which forms a part of them; a transverse buccal orifice at the extremity of a kind of cavity, at the bottom of which is the true mouth between two thick vertical lips; a lingual band bristled with small teeth and prolonged into the abdomen.

*Shell.* Oval, convex, very smooth, involute; spire entirely posterior, very small, often concealed by a calcareous layer deposited by the lobes of the mantle; aperture longitudinal, very narrow, slightly arcuated, as long as the shell and with the edges internally dentated, and notched at each extremity. Inhabits the W. Indian seas and Sandwich Islands. One hundred and eighteen species.

Cypræa princeps.

C. mappa.

C. tigris.

C. pantherina.

C. mauritania.

C. stercararia.

C. aurora.

C. leucodon.

C. sulcidentata.

C. Arabica.

C. lynx.

C. vitellus.

C. carneola.

C. cinerea.

C. Reevi.

C. obscurus.

C. achatina.

C. arenosa.

C. nivosa.

C. Broderipii.

C. exanthema.

C. cervus.

C. testudinaria.

C. talpa.

C. exusta.

Cypræa dediculus.

C. oryza.

C. coccinella.

C. Australis.

C. Childrini.

C. depauparata.

C. solandri.

C. Californica.

C. suffusa.

C. pacifica.

C. pediculus.

C. nivea.

C. oryxa.

C. stercus-muscarum.

C. pulex.

C. fusca.

C. Europea.

C. sanguinea.

C. quadripunctata.

C. rufescens.

C. maugeriæ.

C. aperta.

C. Adansonii.

C. caput-serpentis.

C. Lamarchii.

C. argus.

C. scurra.

C. pulchra.

C. Isabella.

C. controversa.

C. lurida.

C. microdon.

C. Scottii.

C. mus.

C. tessellata.

C. annulata.

C. margarita.

C. cicercula.

C. globulus.

C. staphylæa.

C. tigrina.

C. cerina.

C. Argus.

C. histrio.

C. alba.

C. zonata.

C. icterina.

C. lota.

C. ovulata.

C. helvola.

C. Arabicula.

C. pustulata.

C. nucleus.

C. limacina.

C. moneta.

C. obvelata.

C. annulus.

C. radians.

C. oniscus.

C. Cumingii.

C. Goodalii.

C. Humphreysii.

C. Walkeri.

C. Listeri.

C. pulchella.

C. pyriformis.

C. piperita.

C. algoensis.

C. edentula.

C. similis.

C. fusco-dentata.

C. gangrenosa.

C. bicallosa.

C. poraria.

C. guttata.

C. Xanthodon.

C. nigro-punctata.

C. pallida.

C. zigzag.

C. moneta.

C. aurantia.

C. fimbriata.

C. variolaria.

C. erosa.

C. miliaris.

C. ratta.

C. asella.

C. turda.

C. adusta.

C. moniliaris.

C. ursella.

C. hirundo.

C. olivacea.

2. Genus *Ovula.* Pl. XII.

*Animal.* As above.

*Shell.* Oblong, convex, distinguished from the Cypræa by the want of a spire, and by not having teeth on the columellar lip; the two extremities of the aperture notched, and more or less prolonged like a tube; left margin dentated. Inhabits the Indian seas. Twelve species.

| | |
|---|---|
| Ovula oviformis. | Ovula carnea. |
| O. verrucosa, | O. gibbosa. |
| O. spelta. | O. volva. |
| O. angulosa. | O. lactea. |
| O. hordacea. | O. triticea. |
| O. birostris. | O. acicularis. |

### 3. Genus *Terebellum.* Pl. XII.

*Animal.* Entirely unknown.

*Shell.* Thin, shining, subcylindrical, involute, pointed posteriorly, truncated anteriorly; aperture longitudinal, triangular; edges entire, columella truncated and prolonged beyond the aperture. Inhabits the Indian Ocean. One living species and two fossil.

Terebellum subulatum.

### 4. Genus *Ancillaria.* Pl. XII.

*Animal.* Unknown.

*Shell.* Smooth, oval, oblong, posteriorly, widened and truncated anteriorly; aperture oval, somewhat elongated, angular posteriorly; a wide but not deep slope anteriorly; columella covered anteriorly with an oblique callous band; right lip obtuse. Inhabits the Australian seas. Four living species, and five fossil.

| | |
|---|---|
| Ancillaria cinnamonea. | Ancillaria candida. |
| A. ventricosa. | A. marginata. |

### 5. Genus *Oliva.* Pl. XII.

*Animal.* Oval, involute, mouth somewhat thin at its edges, prolonged to the two angles of the branchial aperture in a tentacular band, and, anteriorly, by a long branchial tube; foot very large, oval, subauriculated, with a transverse cleft anteriorly; head small with a labial proboscis.

*Shell.* Thick, solid, smooth, oval, elongated, subcylindrical, the whorls of the spire very small and separated by a canal; aperture long and narrow, the columellar edge dilated anteriorly by a band striated obliquely in all its length. Found in the Australian and Equatorial seas. Sixty-two species. Six fossil.

| | |
|---|---|
| Oliva textilina. | Oliva reticularis. |
| O. pica. | O. granitella. |
| O. angulata. | O. literata. |
| O. cepulturalis. | O. tricolor. |
| O. irrisans. | O. mustelina. |
| O. episcopalis. | O. funebralis. |
| O. venulata. | O. Peruviana. |
| O. leucophœa. | O. fusiformis. |
| O. inflata. | O. acuminata. |
| O. harpularia. | O. luteola. |
| O. ustulata. | O. hiatula. |
| O. tessellata. | O. Ceylonica. |
| O. espidula. | O. fabagina. |
| O. candida. | O. undatella. |
| O. tigrina. | O. nana. |
| O. utricula. | O. oryza. |
| O. porphyria. | O. flammulata. |
| O. erythrostoma. | O. araneosa. |
| O. themulina. | O. scripta. |
| O. maura. | O. sanguinolenta. |
| O. fulminans. | O. lugubris. |
| O. elegans. | O. glandiformis. |
| O. guttata. | O. senagalensis. |
| O. undata. | O. auricularis. |
| O. bicincta. | O. subulata. |
| O. hepatica. | O. testacca. |
| O. avellana. | O. obtusaria. |
| O. carneola. | O. nebulosa. |
| O. oriola. | O. conordalis. |
| O. volutella. | O. eburnea. |
| O. Brazilliana. | O. Zonalis. |

### 6. Genus *Conus.*   Pl. XII.

*Animal.* Elongated, much compressed, involute; foot small, oval, long, widest in front, where it is edged by a transverse furrow; head tolerably distinct; tentacula cylindrical, having the eyes near their summit, which is setaceous; mouth at the bottom of a long labial trunk; a somewhat short tongue, although projecting into the visceral cavity, and bristled with long styliform hooks in two rows.

*Shell.* Covered with a periosteal membrane, thick, solid, involute, conical; summit of the cone anterior, spire slightly projecting, or not at all; a very narrow longitudinal aperture; external edge straight and trenchant; the internal also straight with oblique folds in its anterior portion; a very small horny operculum, subspirated, with a terminal summit. Found in the Australian and Mediterranean seas. One hundred and eighty-one species.

| | |
|---|---|
| Conus Bandanus. | Conus betulinus. |
| C. Nicobaricus. | C. puncticulatus. |
| C. zonatus. | C. Proteus. |
| C. fuscatus. | C. augur. |
| C. regius. | C. nivosus. |
| C. marmoreus. | C. acuminatus. |
| C. nocturnus. | C. Janus. |
| C. araneosus. | C. lithoglyphus. |
| C. imperialis. | C. venulatus. |
| C. viridulus. | C. muscosus. |
| C. tulipa. | C. Mozambicus. |
| C. punctatus. | C. Franciscanus. |
| C. musicus. | C. rattus. |
| C. mus. | C. amabilis. |
| C. Barbadensis. | C. nobilis. |
| C. geographicus. | C. terminus. |
| C. tæniatus. | C. gubernator. |
| C. miliaris. | C. terebra. |
| C. lividus. | C. raphanus. |
| C. roseus. | C. spectrum. |
| C. cedo-nulli. | C. leoninus. |
| C. nebulosus. | C. pertusus. |

C. suleatus.

C. vermiculatus.

C. pulicarius.

C. obesus.

C. millepunctatus.

C. eburneus.

C. generalis.

C. Malacanus.

C. monile.

C. vitulinus.

C. flavidus.

C. dancus.

C. capitaneus.

C. vittatus.

C. vexillus.

C. figulinus.

C. aurantius.

C. minimus.

C. Hebræus.

C. arenatus.

C. fustigatus.

C. varius.

C. literatus.

C. tesselatus.

C. Maldivus.

C. lineatus.

C. centurio.

C. vulpinus.

C. virgo.

C. pastinacus.

C. classiarius.

C. mustelinus.

C. Sumatrensis.

C. quercinus.

C. cardinalis.

C. distans.

C. Caledonicus.

C. fulgurans.

C. amadis.

C. flammeus.

C. testiludinarius.

C. quæstor.

C. Narcissus.

C. Guniaicus.

C. informis.

C. Jamaicensis.

C. Omaicus.

C. aurisiacus.

C. striatus.

C. grannulatus.

C. verulosus.

C. magus.

C. Bullatus.

C. auratus.

C. omaria.

C. panniculus.

C. Timorensis.

C. præfectus.

C. nimbosus.

C. archiepiscopus.

C. legatus.

C. canonicus.

C. textilis.

C. australis.

C. Mauritianus.

C. eques.

C. catus.

C. acutangulus.

C. Japonicus.

C. columba.

C. nemocanus.

C. fusiformis.

C. Aurora.

C. Adansonii.

C. puncturatus.
C. lamellosus.
C. exiguus.
C. hyæna.
C. ammiralis.
C. papilionaceus.
C. Prometheus.
C. Suratensis.
C. ranunculus.
C. achatinus.
C. stramineus.
C. lacteus.
C. vicarius.
C. orchraceus.
C. Mediterraneus.
C. Magellanicus.
C. pontificalis.
C. sponsalis.
C. Ceylonensis.
C. pusillus.
C. asper.
C. miles.
C. genuanus.
C. siamensis.
C. glaucus.
C. monachus.
C. anemone.
C. cinereus.
C. zebra.
C. cingulatus.
C. mercator.

C. Portoricanus.
C. strigatus.
C. mitratus.
C. aulicus.
C. colubrinus.
C. auricomus.
C. rubiginosus.
C. prælatus.
C. fumigatus.
C. luzonicus.
C. verrucosus.
C. mindanus.
C. pusio.
C. madurensis.
C. cancellatus.
C. cærulescens.
C. Taitensis.
C. tinianus.
C. crocatus.
C. glans.
C. nussatella.
C. clavous.
C. pennaceus.
C. cervus.
C. dux.
C. stercus-muscarum.
C. tendineus.
C. melancholicus.
C. episcopus.
C. pyramidalis.
C. abbas.

C. gloria-maris.

## FAMILY XXII.

NAUTILACEA. Two genera.

1. Genus *Spirula.* Pl. XII.

*Animal.* Body elongated, cylindrical, terminated posteriorly by two lateral lobes partially concealing the shell; head provided with five pairs of tentacula, of which two are longer than the others.

*Shell.* Very symmetrical, longitudinally twisted throughout nearly all its extent; the cone spiral, conical, regular, circular; whorls of the spire very evident; partitions simple, concave, and pierced by a single syphon. Inhabits the West Indian seas. One species.

Spirula Peronii.

## 2. Genus *Nautilus.* Pl. XII.

*Animal.* Body round and terminated posteriorly by a tendinous or muscular filament, attaching itself to the syphon, by which the partitions of the shell are pierced; the mantle opening obliquely, and prolonged into a sort of hood above the head, (which is provided with digitated tentacula) and surrounding the aperture of the mouth.

*Shell.* Discoid, but slightly compressed, with a rounded or subcarenated back, umbilicated or not, but never mamelonated, the partitions simple, not visible exteriorly; the last profoundly sunk and perforated by a syphon running through them all. Inhabits the Indian Ocean. Two living species. Fifteen fossil.

Nautilus Pompilius.          Nautilus Umbilicatus.

## FAMILY XXIII.

HETEROPODA. Two genera.

## 1. Genus *Argonauta.* Pl. XII.

*Animal.* Body conical, elongated, enrolled longitudinally, widened anteriorly, and provided on each side with an arcuated subtriangular, aliform appendage; mouth at the extremity of the angle formed by two inferior lips. De Blainville denies that this animal is at all known, and speaks of one described by M. Oken as a small polypus of the genus Ocythoe.

*Shell.* Navicular, symmetrical, very thin, compressed, bicari-

14

nated, longitudinally subinvolute in the same plane; aperture very wide, symmetrical, complete, square anteriorly, slightly modified by the turn of the summit, and provided on each side with an earlike appendage having thick and smooth edges. Inhabits the Mediterranean. Three species.

Argonauta argo.  Argonauta tuberculosa.
A. nitida.

## 2. Genus *Carinaria*. Pl. XII.

*Animal.* Body elongated, prolonged behind the nucleus into a veritable tail edged at its extremity by a vertical fin; head sufficiently distinct, two long conical tentacula; two sessile eyes; the organs of respiration and the nucleus entirely enveloped in a mantle with lobed edges.

*Shell.* Very thin, symmetrical, a little compressed, without spire, but with the summit a little reflexed posteriorly; aperture oval and entire. Inhabits the African, Mediterranean, and Australian seas. Three species.

Carinaria vitrea.  Carinaria fragilis.
C. cymbia.

# GLOSSARY

## OF TERMS USED IN CONCHOLOGY.

### A.

Abbreviated, cut short.

Abdomen, the belly.

Acuminated, sharp pointed.

Aculeated, prickly.

Alated, winged.

Annulated, divided into rings.

Annulations, rings.

Aperture, the orifice or opening of the shell.

Apex, the point of the spire.

Approximating, approaching together.

Arcuated, of an arch form.

Area, surface between the lines.

Articulations, junctures or joints.

Attenuated, thin, slender.

Aurated, having ears, as the Pecten.

Auricled, having ear-like appendages.

Auriform, ear shaped.

### B.

Barbed, bearded.

Base, lower extremity of the shell.

Beak, prolongation at the base.

Beard, see Byssus,

Bi, signifying two,

Biangulated, having two corners or angles.

Bidentate, having two teeth.

Bifid, opening with a cleft.

Bilobate, divided into two lobes.

Bimarginate, two margins or lips.

Biradiate, having two rays.

Bivalve, having two valves.

Blunt, obtuse, opposed to acute.

Borer, a piercer.

Bulging, gibbous, swollen out.

Byssus, common in the Mytilus and Pinna, by which they attach themselves to objects.

### C.

Callous, indurated.

Callosity, a protuberance.

Calcareous, relating to lime.

Canal, the prolongation of the beak.

Canaliculated, channelled or grooved.

Cardinal, see Teeth.

Carinated, like a boat's keel.

Cartilage, a flexible fibrous substance by which the valves are united.

Cartilaginous, resembling a ligament.

Chambered, divided by partitions.

Cicatrix, the muscular impression.

Ciliated, edged with bristles or hairs.

Cinerous, of an ash color.

Clavate, club shaped.

Columella, the upright pillar of the shell.

Complicated, doubled together.

Compressed, flattened.

Concave, hollowed out.

Concentric, running to the centre.

Cone, the form of a sugar loaf.

Convolute, whorls turning round.

Confluent, running together.

Conoid, figure like a cone.

Contorted, twisted in oblique direction.

Contracted, shortened, shrunk, up.

Cordate, heart shape.

Cordiform, form of a heart.

Coriaceous, leather-like consistence.

Corneus, resembling horn.

Coronal, resembling a crown.

Coronated, crowned towards the apex.

Costated, ribbed.

Cortex, anterior skin.

Crenulated, notched at the margin.

Crispated, with waving lines.

Cuneform, wedge form.

Cylindrical, round like a roller.

Cybiform, boat-shaped.

### D.

Decollated, truncated transversely.

Decorticated, divested of epidermis.

Decussated, lines intersecting each other.

Deflexed, bent aside.

Dentated, having teeth.

Depressed, shallow, flat.

Diaphanous, clear, pellucid.

Digitated, having finger-like claws.

Disk, the highest part of the valves.

Divaricated, spreading out.

Divergent, tending to a point.

Dorsal, belonging to the back.

Dotted, punctured like a thimble.

Duplicated, divided into plaits or folds.

### E.

Ears, projections on the sides of the hinge.

Echinated, set with spires.

Effuse, spread out.

Elliptical, oval.

Elongated, drawn out.

Emarginated, with the edge notched.

Ensisform, sabre-shaped.

Entire, whole.

Epidermis, the outer coating of a shell.

Equilateral, all sides alike.

Equivalve, both sides alike.

Exserted, protruding.

### F.

Falcated, hooped like a scythe.

Fasciated, covered with bands.

Ferruginous, of an iron color.

Filament, a thread-like process.

Filiform, thread-shaped, slender.

Fimbriated, fringed.

Fissure, a cleft or slit.

Flexuous, zigzag, with angles widening.

Flexure, a bending.

Fluviatile, belonging to fresh water.

Foliaceous, lamina or leave-shaped.

Fragile, brittle, easily broken.

Front, the aperture next the observer.

Furcated, forked.

Furrow, a trench or hollow.

Fuscated, darkened, obscured.

Fusiform, spindle shaped, conical or oval.

## G.

Gaping, when the valves do not close.

Geniculate, keeled.

Genus, characters by which they are distinguished from others.

Genera, plural of genus.

Gibbous, bulged.

Glabrous, having a smooth surface.

Globose, globular, round.

## H.

Hemispherical, in the shape of a half globe.

Heterostrophe, shells whose spires reverse.

Hispid, hairy.

Hinge, the part where the valves are united.

## I. & J.

Jagged, denticulated, uneven.

Imbricate, covered with scales.

Imperforate, having no umbilicus.

Inequilateral, when the anterior and posterior parts of the shell are dissimilar.

Inequivalve, when the valves are dissimilar.

Inarticulate, indistinct.

Incumbent, one lying over the other.

Incurved, bent backward.

Indented, unequally marked.

Inflated, tumid, swollen.

Inflected, bent inward.

Inflexed, bent towards each other.

Intercostal, placed between the ribs.

Interrupted, divided, separated.

Interstice, space between.

Intortion, turning or twisting.

Involute, without a spire.

Involution, that part which involves another.

Juncture, the joining of the whorl in univalves.

## K.

Keel, the longitudinal prominence in the argonauta.

Keeled, see carinated.

## L.

Labra, the lips.

Laciniate, cut in irregular segments.

Lacunose, surface covered with pits.

Lamellar, films on plates.

Lamellated, divided into distinct plaits or foliations.

Laminæ, thin plates, laid one above another.

Lanceolate, oblong, tapering like the head of a lance.

Lateral, extending to one side from the centre.

Latticed, see decussated.

Lenticulate, doubly convex.

Ligament, a solid body which connects the valves in bivalves.

Linear, composed of lines.

Linguiformed, tongue shaped.

Lip, the outer edge of the aperture of univalves.

Lobated, rounded at the edges.

Longitudinal, the length of the shell.

Lunated, formed like a half moon.

Lunule, crescent-like.

Luniform, shape of a crescent.

### M.

Margin, the whole circumference or outline of the shell in bivalves.

Marginated, having a prominent margin or border.

Membrane, a web of fibres.

Mouth, see Aperture.

Muscular impressions, marks made by the animal in adhering to the shell.

Mottled, clouded, or spotted.

Mucronate, ending in a sharp point.

Multilocular, many chambered.

Muricated, clothed with sharp spines.

### N.

Nacred, pearly.

Nemoral, belonging to a wood.

Nited, glossy.

Nodose, knotty.

Nucleus, a kernel.

### O.

Obsolete, obliterated.

Oblong, oval.

Ocellated, eyelike spots.

Ochreous, color of yellow ochre.

Offuscated, darkened, clouded.

Olivaceous, of a greenish olive color.

Operculum, which closes the aperture of the shell.

Orbicular, circular, round.

Orifice, an opening or perforation.

Ovate, shaped like an egg.

Ovoid, oval.

### P.

Papillose, pimpled, dotted.

Papyraceous, thin as paper.

Patulous, with a gap or opening.

Partitions, processes dividing the shells of the Nautilus, Serpula, &c.

Pectinated, resembling the teeth of a comb.

Pedicle, the support of the Anatifera and its corresponding species.

Peduncle, a tube on which any thing is seated.

Pellucid, transparent, clear, bright.

Pentagonal, having five sides.

Perforated, pierced with holes.

Pervious, admitting passage.

Pillar, in univalves the internal continuation of the columella or inner lips, extending from the *base* to the *apex.*

Pinnated, winged.

Plaited, folded.

Plaits, folds.

Plicated, folded or plaited.

Posterior, see Margin.

Produced, lengthened out.

Protrude, to thrust forward.

Punctuated, like the punctures of a thimble.

Pyriform, pear shaped.

### Q.

Quadrangular, having four right angles.

Quadriplicated, having four plaits.

### R.

Radiated, furnished with rays.

Radicated, fixed by the base to another body.

Rectangular, having right angles.

Recurvated, turned backward.

Recurved, bowed back.

Reflected, bent backward.

Refracted, abruptly bent.

Reniform, kidney shaped.

Replicated, folded or plaited.

Reticulated, formed like a piece of net work.

Retuse, ending in an obtuse sinus.

Reversed spire, see heterostrophe.

Revolute, rolled backward.

Ribbed, having longitudinal ribs.

Ridge, the upper part of a slope.

Rostrum, the beak.

Rugose, wrinkled.

### S.

Sanguinaceous, divided into chambers.

Scabious, rough, rugged.

Scalloped, indented at the edges.

Scuttelated, shield shaped.

Seam, line formed by the union of the valves.

Semi, the half.

Semi-cordate, half heart shaped.

Semi-orbicular, shape of a half globe.

Semi-lunar, shape of half moon.

Septiform, shape of a partition.

Serrated, like the teeth of a saw.

Sessile, sitting or seated.

Seta, a bristle.

Setaceous, covered with bristles.

Setiferous, bearing bristles.

Sinister valve, is the left valve.

Sinus, a groove or cavity.

Siphunculus, a cylindrical perforation as in the Nautilus, Spirula, &c.

Spatulate, rounded and broad at the top.

Species, the division of a family or genus.

Spiny, thorny.

Spinous, like a hedgehog.

Spire, all the whorls in univalves except the one in which the aperture is situated, which is termed the body.

Spiral, twisted like a corkscrew.

Squamose, scaly.

Striated, covered with thread-like lines.

Sub, almost.

Subarcuated, somewhat arched.

Subconic, somewhat conical.

Subulate, awlshaped.

Sulcated, furrowed.

Summit, the tip or apex.

Suture, a hollow line of division in univalves, the spiral line of which separates the wreaths.

### T.

Teeth, pointed protuberances within the hinge in bivalves, by which the valves are united.

Tentacula, the feelers of snails, which inhabit shells.

Tessalated, checquered like a chess board.

Testacea, that order of animals covered with a testaceous shell.

Testaceous, consisting of carbonate of lime and animal matter.

Tortuosity, flexure.

Tortuous, twisted.

Transverse, crossways.

Trapeziform, shaped like a trapezium.

Trigonel, having three angles.

Truncated, cut short, ending abruptly.

Tubercle, knot or pimple.

Tuberculated, knotted, pimpled.

Tubular, in the shape of a hollow tube.

Tunicated, coated.

Turbinated, shape like a top or pear.

Turgid, swollen.

### U and V.

Valves, the various pieces which compose the shell.

Varices, longitudinal ribs in univalve shells.

Variety, difference in species.

Vaulted, roofed.

Ventral, belonging to the belly.

Ventricose, inflated, swelled in the middle.

Vermiform, worm shaped.

Vertex, the top or most prominent part.

Verrucose, warted.

Verticulated, whorled.

Umbilicated, having a depression in the centre.

Umbo, the round part which turns over the hinge.

Undulated, waved.

Ungulate, shaped like a horse's hoof.

Unilocular, chambered singly.

Univalve, shells of one valve only.

Volutions, the turnings of univalves.

### W.

Whorl, a spiral convolution.

### Z.

Zigzag, having reverse turnings and windings.

Zoned, surrounded by belts or girdles.

**THE END.**

# INDEX.